STUDY GUIDE
Alastair Younger
University of Ottawa

PSYCHOLOGY
Brain, Behavior, & Culture

Third Edition

Drew Westen
Boston University

JOHN WILEY & SONS, INC.

COVER PHOTO: "Ideal Woman" by Robert Silvers.

To order books or for customer service call 1-800-CALL-WILEY (225-5945).

ISBN 0-471-41597-9

Printed in the United States of America.

10 9 8 7 6 5 4 3

Printed and bound by Courier Kendallville, Inc.

Contents

Preface
How to Use This Study Guide

Congratulations on having purchased the study guide to accompany *Psychology: Brain, Behavior, and Culture, Third Edition* by Drew Westen. The purpose of this guide is to get you actively involved in learning the material in your textbook. Its goal is to help you better understand and apply the concepts from the book. Proper use of the study guide, therefore, will enhance your learning of psychology as it is delineated in this well-written textbook by Westen.

The study guide has been designed to facilitate *active* learning. For many students, learning and studying are all-too-often passive rather than active processes. Attending class, reading the textbook, and so on, are, of course, important parts of learning, but most of these activities place students in the role of passive recipient of knowledge rather than active participant in learning. Even when studying, many students simply reread what they have highlighted, recopy their notes, and so on. These strategies lack active integration of knowledge and diagnostic testing of information.

By contrast, active learning requires that students take control of the learning process. Taking control of the learning process means studying in a manner that facilitates *learning*, not superficial memorization. Specifically, actively learning psychology from your Westen textbook requires previewing your textbook to identify exactly where the book and the course are going, pre-reading each chapter before you read it so you can maximize your reading comprehension, working the chapter as opposed to simply reading it, reviewing what you have learned after you read a chapter, and testing your knowledge on an on-going basis so that it becomes committed to memory.

This study guide provides you with specific guidelines for previewing the textbook, pre-reading and working each chapter, and reviewing what you have learned. It also incorporates a variety of diagnostic exercises that will enable you to evaluate what you have learned and "zero in" on areas in which you need to improve. Finally, it outlines an effective method for exam preparation based on the knowledge you have garnered from working through this guide.

The following outline details exactly how to get the most out of this study guide and the Westen psychology text. Take the time to read through each point and incorporate the suggestions. Most of all, enjoy learning about psychology!

Preview The Textbook

How often have you skipped over all the introductory stuff in a textbook and instead started reading chapter one so you could "get to it." Believe it or not, there is a reason for all that introductory stuff, and skipping it makes learning the content of the book harder. Before you begin reading chapter one, take a little time to preview the book. Begin by reading the author's preface. It will tell you how the book is laid out, why it's laid out that way, and what to expect in each chapter.

Next, read the detailed table of contents so you can see what the author was talking about. Take out your course syllabus and compare it to the table of contents. How does your professor plan to use the textbook? Will you be covering one chapter per week, one chapter per class, or multiple chapters per class? Do you need to know a chapter inside-and-out before class so you can discuss it, or are you reading the textbook as supplemental material to topics covered in class? When will you be tested? Can you tell from the syllabus how many chapters are covered on an exam? Mark dates and as much information as you can on the table of contents so you know exactly when you need to do what.

Combine this information to create a "time line" of the semester. You may even wish to create a master calendar of all your courses, so you can determine crunch times, etc. Let's face it—in a perfect world, you would study as little as possible to learn as much as you can. Doing a little work up front will enable you to balance all the stuff you have going on, do well in your courses, and still have time for an occasional social activity.

Chapter By Chapter

There are three parts to actively learning each chapter. First, **pre-read and work** the chapter. Second, **review and learn** the content. Third, **test and know** the material.

Pre-read and Work

Why is it easier to read about a subject with which you are familiar than about a totally foreign topic? The more you know about something, the easier it is for your brain to process related information (after studying chapters 3-6, you'll know exactly why this is true). Therefore, to get the most out of your reading, you need to know—before you read it—what it's going to be about. If you read a chapter without having any idea what's going to be covered or what important information will show up, it will be easy to get lost in the details of the chapter and miss the salient points. Also, it is very difficult upon first read to comprehend complex material that's full of unfamiliar jargon. Therefore, to maximize your reading, pre-read each chapter so you recognize important stuff when you come to it.

How do you pre-read a chapter? First, open to the appropriate chapter in the book and corresponding study guide chapter. Carefully read the table of contents at the front of the chapter in the book. Then flip to the summary at the end of the chapter and carefully read each point. This will give you a good idea of the important points of this chapter . Although you won't remember all these points, you will recognize many of them when you read the chapter. This recognition will enhance your ability to assimilate the important information in the chapter more quickly.

Now you are ready to begin to "work" the first segment of the chapter. (Note: If a segment is long or covers particularly dense material, you may wish to read the author's interim summary before you read the segment). Working a segment means actively reading while keeping an eye on what you are trying to glean from the text. As you read, jot down your questions, comments, and notes in the space provided in the **Outline** section of the study guide, and make note of the important terms you come across. Include page numbers of and references to difficult material that you know you will need to review. After you have finished your reading, turn to the **Learning Objectives**. These objectives take the form of short-answer questions. After reading the chapter, check off the questions you are confident that you can answer well. Review the material in the textbook for the questions about which you are less confident, recording the important points from your reading in the space below each question.

Review and Learn

After you finish working a chapter, you need to take time to really learn the material. This cannot be done immediately after you read the chapter. If possible, wait a day and then review the content of the chapter you read. If you need to do it all in one night, take a break or do some other homework that is completely different from this text.

To review a chapter, reread your answers to the learning objectives questions and key terms, plus your notes. Flip back to any parts of the text about which you feel less-than-confident and reread them. Also, reread the author's interim summaries and end-of-chapter summaries. Mark any areas that seem difficult or confusing to you so you can review them again in the future.

Once you have reviewed the material, apply your knowledge *without referring back to the textbook*. Define the **Key Terms** and do the **Fill-in Exercises**. Then, do the **Application** and **Using What You Have Learned** exercises.

As you work, mark any of the terms or questions that give you difficulty. Once you have finished an exercise, go back to your notes to find answers to the questions that gave you trouble. If you need to, go back to the textbook to find the answers. Finally, check your terms by flipping through the textbook or reading the end-of-chapter summary. All the key terms in the study guide are in **bold** in the text, and are also listed at the end of each chapter in the text. Answers to the fill-ins are found in the answer key in the study guide.

Why should you find the answers to difficult questions on your own as opposed to checking the answer key? The idea of these exercises is to help you commit this information to memory, to really *learn* the content of the chapter. If you were to simply check your work against an answer key, you would not be actively learning. The more clear you are about *why* an answer is right, the more likely you are to understand and remember it. This goes for questions you answered correctly by virtue of a "lucky guess." If you guessed on a question, mark it as a guess and verify it by looking back to your notes and the textbook.

Test and Know

On a separate day (preferably after some period of time has lapsed), test yourself using the **Sample Questions**. You may wish to mark your answers on a separate sheet of paper, and take this test again before you have an exam in class (see "Exam Review Strategy" later in this chapter for more exam prep ideas). Again, when you check your answers, review the information thoroughly. Getting questions right is good; knowing why they are right is better.

Upon completing these three parts to active learning, the information contained in a chapter will be stuff you *know*, not stuff you have temporarily memorized for a test. As you work through subsequent chapters, go back and review parts of earlier chapters as needed. The chapters in your textbook build on each other, so reviewing earlier concepts will be easy. If you continually review the concepts you have learned, you won't need to "cram for the exam," because you will know most of the information cold. You may need to review complicated concepts and terms, but you shouldn't need to reread the basic stuff.

Sounds like an awful lot of work, right? Active learning does require more effort. However, imagine instead taking a passive approach to learning this stuff. You read the book. You highlight stuff. Midterms come and you have nine chapters (over 350 pages) of stuff to reread and relearn in one day to be ready for the exam, not to mention that you also have four other major courses to cram for and tickets to the concert of the year. Active learning requires more investment up front, but pays off big in the end. Given that you have to read the stuff anyway, why not take the time to learn it the first time?

Exam Review Strategy

If you have consistently worked with this study guide, exam preparation will involve:
- Testing yourself
- Reviewing your notes on each chapter
- Reviewing tricky terms
- Rereading difficult segments (previously indicated by you)
- Rereading the interim summaries and end-of-chapter summaries
- Testing yourself

First test how well you have learned the information by giving yourself a mini-exam. To create a mini-exam, rework the Key Terms, Learning Objectives, and Sample Questions for each chapter (cover your answers or have a friend ask you the questions).

Once you take the mini-exam, you will know exactly how much studying you need to do. Review and reread what you need to (for the most thorough review, follow the outline above). This review shouldn't take long since you've done all the pre-work. After you finish your review, take your mini-exam again, or have a classmate "quiz you" on stuff from the chapters in the textbook. Then, go ace that exam!

Hopefully you will find this study guide a useful tool which enables you to truly learn psychology as it is presented in your textbook. Good luck in your course. This is a great psychology text—enjoy learning about psychology!

Chapter 1
Psychology: The Study of Mental Processes and Behavior

PART ONE: PRE-READ AND WORK
Outline and Learning Objectives

Pre-read this chapter's table of contents and end-of-chapter summary. Then, use the outline segment-by-segment to help you work through the chapter. Jot down your own questions, comments, and notes in the space provided. Make a note of key terms and of difficult areas that you will need to review (include page numbers). Then, answer the questions in the learning objectives section that follows. Check off those you are confident that you can answer well. Re-read the material in the text for the questions about which you are less confident. Record the important points from your reading in the space below each question.

OUTLINE

The Boundaries and Borders of Psychology

From Brain to Behavior: The Boundary with Biology

A Global Vista: The Boundary with Culture

From Philosophy to Psychology

Perspectives in Psychology

The Psychodynamic Perspective

The Behaviorist Perspective

The Cognitive Perspective

The Evolutionary Perspective

Commentary: Putting Psychological Perspectives in Perspective

Central Questions: Facts, Theories, and Perspectives in Psychology

LEARNING OBJECTIVES

Upon completion of Chapter 1, you should be able to answer the following questions.

1.   What is the issue of localization of function in the brain?

2.   What are the two types of aphasias described by Paul Broca and Carl Wernicke?

3.   What are the similarities and differences between psychological anthropology and cross-cultural psychology?

4.   How are both free-will and determinism evident in much of a person's behavior and characteristics?

5.   Discuss eight fundamental philosophical questions that set the stage for psychology and are central to contemporary psychological theory and research.

6.   In what ways did functionalism differ from structuralism?

7.   What are the three key components of a paradigm?

8.   According to Kuhn, how do the social sciences differ from the natural sciences?

9.   What are the three key premises of the psychodynamic perspective?

10.   Briefly describe the methods and data of the psychodynamic perspective.

11.   In what ways does the behaviorist perspective differ from Decartes's philosophical perspective?

12.   How does the behaviorist view of the subject matter and research methods of psychology differ from that of the psychodynamic and structuralist schools of thought?

13.   Why has behaviorism sometimes been called "black-box" psychology?

14.   How do cognitive psychologists employ the metaphor of the computer to understand and model the way the mind works?

15.   What are the similarities and differences between the behaviorist perspective and the cognitive perspective?

16.   Briefly explain the relation between adaptation and niches.

17.   Why have many psychologists from other perspectives challenged the research methods commonly used by evolutionary psychologists?

18.   Outline the various subdisciplines of psychology and the types of questions asked by each.

PART TWO: REVIEW AND LEARN
Key Terms, Fill-In Exercises, Application and Using What You Have Learned

Before doing the exercises below, review the information you learned in this chapter. Reread the work you did in part one of this study guide chapter, plus the interim summaries and end-of-chapter summary in your textbook. Review any problem areas. Once you feel comfortable with the material, do the following exercises without referring to your notes or textbook. If you have difficulty with a term or question, mark it and come back to it. When you have finished an exercise, go back to your notes and the textbook to find the answers to the questions that gave you difficulty. Finally, check your answers (key terms against the textbook and the rest against the answer key).

KEY TERMS

Psychology   _____

_____

Biopsychology (or Behavioral neuroscience) _____

_____

Localization of function _____

_____

Psychological anthropologists _____

_____

Cross-cultural psychology _____

_____

Free will versus determinism _____

_____

Mind-body problem _____

_____

Introspection _____

_____

Structuralism _____

_____

Functionalism _____

_____

Paradigm _____

_____

Perspective _____

_____

Psychodynamics   _____

_____

Psychodynamic perspective   _____

_____

Behaviorist perspective   _____

_____

Behaviorism   _____

_____

Cartesian dualism   _____

_____

Cognitive perspective   _____

_____

Cognition   _____

_____

Information processing   _____

_____

Rationalist philosophers_____

_____

Evolutionary perspective_____

_____

Nature-nurture controversy   _____

_____

Natural selection   _____

_____

Adaptive traits   _____

_____

Ethology   _____

_____

Sociobiology   _____

_____

Evolutionary psychologists   _____

_____

Behavioral genetics   _____

_____

Reproductive success   _____

_____

Inclusive fitness   _____

_____

Empiricism   _____

_____

Gestalt psychology   _____

_____

FILL-IN EXERCISES

Fill in the word or words that best fit in the spaces below.

1. The degree to which inborn processes determine human behavior is a classic issue in psychology, called the _____-_____ controversy.

2. The attempt to understand the way conscious sensations, feelings, and images fit together was emphasized by an early school of thought known as _____.

3. Wilhelm Wundt, viewed by some as the _____ of psychology, emphasized a research method known as _____, in which trained subjects verbally reported everything that went through their minds when presented with a stimulus or task.

4. Freud argued that people have powerful _____ motives that underlie their conscious intentions.

5. The psychodynamic perspective relies substantially on the _____-_____ method, which entails in-depth observation of a small number of people.

6. John Locke, the seventeenth century British philosopher, contended that at birth the mind is a _____ _____ upon which experience writes itself.

7. Behaviorism focuses on the way objects or events in the environment, referred to as _____, come to control behavior through learning.

8. Skinner observed that the behaviors of organisms can be controlled by environmental conditions that either _____ or _____ their likelihood of occurring.

9. Many behaviorists view the mind as a _____ _____ whose mechanisms can never be observed.

10. The primary method of behaviorism is the _____ method.

11. Many cognitive psychologists use the metaphor of the computer to understand and model the way the mind works. From this perspective, thinking is _____ _____.

12. In contrast to the behaviorists, cognitive psychologists have shown _____ (*more/less*) interest in the questions raised by Descartes and other rationalist philosophers.

13. As with behaviorism, the primary method of the cognitive perspective is _____, but with one important difference: Cognitive psychologists use such procedures to infer _____ processes at work.

14.   The theory of natural selection suggests that natural forces select traits in organisms that are _____ and are likely to be passed on to their offspring.

15.   The fundamental concept in all contemporary evolutionary theories is that evolution selects organisms that maximize their _____ success.

16.   Organisms with fewer adaptive features for their particular _____, or environmental circumstance, are less likely to survive and reproduce.

17.   Conrad Lorenz hypothesized that jackdaws have an _____ (i.e., inborn) tendency to become distressed whenever they see a creature dangling a black object resembling a jackdaw.

18.   _____ refers to the belief that the road to scientific knowledge is systematic observation, and ideally experimental observation.

19.   The field of study that examines interactions of individual psychology and social phenomena is referred to as _____ _____.

USING WHAT YOU HAVE LEARNED

Chapter 1 presents four theoretical perspectives in psychology: psychodynamic, behaviorist, cognitive, and evolutionary. At first each seems to conflict with the others. Yet, as the author points out, often one approach complements another -- asks questions the other approach overlooks or adds information not addressed by the other approach. Spend some time reviewing each approach. Can you see their complementarity?

Try applying each approach to some aspect of your own life. Think, for example, about how you responded in a particular situation recently.

1.   Can you imagine the role of unconscious desires or attitudes, or some long forgotten conflict from your childhood (the psychodynamic perspective) influencing your behavior?

2.   What about prior experience? How does your experience with similar situations and the consequences associated with similar behavior (the behaviorist perspective) influence your current behavior?

3.   Consider how you interpret the circumstances surrounding your behavior, how others react to you, what you pay attention to in their reactions, and so on (the cognitive perspective).

4.   Finally, can you see any possible survival value in your behavior (the evolutionary perspective). If not, could it be that this behavior might have been adaptive in a different niche?

APPLICATION

Consider the following explanations for anxiety. Which theory would be best associated with each explanation?

1.   At one point in time, anxiety was very adaptive, as it prepared us to either fight or flee from situations where real danger was present. In our current society, often neither fighting nor fleeing is a viable option.

2.   Anxiety comes about because certain environmental stimuli have been associated with negative or harmful consequences. The stimulus, therefore, comes to trigger an automatic fear response.

3.   Anxiety comes about because we develop negative expectations about what will likely happen in a particular situation. These expectations cause us to pay close attention to signs of potential harm and to process such information more easily than other information around us.

4.   Anxiety may come about from wishes or fears that we have put out of conscious awareness. We may not even be aware of why we are anxious.

PART THREE: TEST AND KNOW
SAMPLE TEST QUESTIONS

Test how well you have learned this chapter's material by answering the sample test questions. You may wish to mark your answers on a separate sheet of paper so you can reuse this test for exam review. Once you have completed the exam, check your answers and then go back to your notes and the textbook to review questions you found difficult.

1.   To understand an individual at a given point in time, psychologists must track

   a.   biological events
   b.   psychological experience
   c.   the cultural and historical context
   d.   all of the above

2.   Paul Broca observed that individuals with lesions in the front section of the left hemisphere

   a.   were able to speak fluently but could not comprehend language
   b.   could both speak fluently and comprehend well
   c.   were unable to comprehend language or speak comprehensibly
   d.   were often unable to speak fluently but could comprehend language

3.   Cross-cultural psychologists

a.   attempt to distinguish universal psychological processes from those that are specific to particular cultures.
b.   argue that the only important findings concerning psychological processes are those that hold true across cultures.
c.   believe that all psychological processes are culturally specific; nothing is universal.
d.   assert that all psychological processes involve an equal balance between the individual and his or her culture.

4.   "Do we freely choose our actions, or is our behavior caused by things outside our control?" This philosophical view is know as

a.   rationalism versus empiricism
b.   individualism versus relationality
c.   free will versus determinism
d.   nature versus nurture

5.   Whereas Wundt and Tichener were associated with the structuralist school of psychology, William James was a _____.

a.   sociobiologist   b.   psychoanalyst
c.   functionalist   d.   behaviorist

6.   Which of the following is not a key component of a paradigm?

a.   It includes a set of findings that will be considered acceptable by the scientific community.
b.   It includes a set of theoretical assertions that provide a model of the object of study.
c.   It includes a set of shared metaphors that compare the object under investigation to something else that is readily apprehended.
d.   It includes a set of methods that members of the scientific community agree will, if properly executed, provide valid and useful data.

7.   According to Kuhn, the social sciences differ from the older natural sciences in that

a.   social sciences lack an accepted paradigm upon which most members of the scientific community agree
b.   although they have an accepted paradigm upon which most members of the scientific community agree, social scientists tend to align themselves with one of several different perspectives
c.   there are a limited number of perspectives in the social sciences, whereas the number in the natural sciences seems unlimited
d.   social sciences borrow perspectives from the natural sciences, whereas the natural sciences never borrow from the social sciences

8.   The relationship between conscious awareness and unconscious mental forces can be considered analogous to the visible tip of an iceberg and the vast, submerged hulk that lies out of sight beneath the water. This notion best fits with which of the following perspectives?

a.   psychodynamic   b.   behaviorist
c.   cognitive   d.   evolutionary

9.   Which of the following research methods is most associated with the psychodynamic perspective?

a.   experimentation   b.   introspection
c.   case study   d.   observation

10.   The notion that the mind at birth can be considered a "tabula rasa" is attributable to

a.   John Locke   b.   B. F. Skinner
c.   Ivan Pavlov   d.   Rene Descartes

11.   Behaviorists argued that

a.   behavior must be considered in the context of motives and goals
b.   behavior can be understood entirely without reference to thoughts and feelings
c.   the science of psychology must emphasize the role of psychological processes in helping individuals adapt to their environment
d.   researchers should apply direct observational methods when studying the structure of consciousness

12.   The notion of the mind as a "black box" is associated with which view?

a.   information processing
b.   structuralism
c.   psychodynamic
d.   behavioral

13.   The primary method of the behaviorist approach is

a.   introspection
b.   deduction
c.   determinism
d.   experimentation

14.   The notion of "information processing" is most associated with which perspective?

a.   evolutionary   b.   structuralist
c.   cognitive   d.   behaviorist

15.   The primary method of the cognitive perspective is

    a.   introspection   b.   deduction
    c.   case study   d.   experimentation

16.   Many, if not most, psychological processes

    a.   are predominantly attributable to environmental influences
    b.   reflect predominantly the influence of innate, biological processes
    c.   reflect an interaction between nature and nurture
    d.   are primarily learned, and not biologically ordained

17.   The field of science that studies animal behavior from a biological and evolutionary perspective is

    a.   sociobiology
    b.   ethology
    c.   behavioral genetics
    d.   anthropological psychology

18.   Behavioral genetics

    a.   refers to an organism's capacity to survive and produce offspring
    b.   is the study of animal behavior from a biological and evolutionary perspective
    c.   explores possible evolutionary and biological bases of human social behavior
    d.   examines the genetic and environmental bases of differences among individuals on psychological traits

19.   Psychologists interested in such phenomena as prejudice, aggression, and groups would most likely be classified as _____ psychologists.

    a.   clinical
    b.   health
    c.   industrial/organizational
    d.   social

20.   The notion that perception involves imposing order on an overwhelming panorama of details by seeing them as parts of larger wholes, was held by

    a.   the structuralists
    b.   psychodynamic psychologists
    c.   Gestalt psychologists
    d.   the functionalists

ANSWERS

FILL-IN EXERCISES

1. nature-nurture   2. structuralism 3. father; introspection   4. unconscious 5. case-study 6. tabula rasa 7. stimuli   8. increase (reinforce); decrease (punish)   9. black box 10. experimental   11. information processing 12. more 13. experimental; mental   14. adaptive 15. reproductive   16. niche   17. innate 18. empiricism   19. social psychology

APPLICATION

1. Evolutionary perspective
2. Behaviorist perspective
3. Cognitive perspective
4. Psychodynamic perspective

SAMPLE TEST QUESTIONS

1.	d	11.	b
2.	d	12.	d
3.	a	13.	d
4.	c	14.	c
5.	c	15.	d
6.	a	16.	c
7.	a	17.	b
8.	a	18.	d
9.	c	19.	d
10.	a	20.	c

Chapter 2
Research Methods
in Psychology

PART ONE: PRE-READ AND WORK
Outline and Learning Objectives

Pre-read this chapter's table of contents and end-of-chapter summary. Then, use the outline segment-by-segment to help you work through the chapter. Jot down your own questions, comments, and notes in the space provided. Make a note of key terms and of difficult areas that you will need to review (include page numbers). Then, answer the questions in the learning objectives section that follows. Check off those you are confident that you can answer well. Re-read the material in the text for the questions about which you are less confident. Record the important points from your reading in the space below each question.

OUTLINE

Characteristics of Good Psychological Research

Theoretical Framework

Standardized Procedures

Generalizability from a Sample

Objective Measurement

Experimental Research

The Logic Of Experimentation

Steps in Conducting Research

Limitations of Experimental Research

Descriptive Research

Case Study Methods

Naturalistic Observation

Survey Research

Correlational Research

From Brain to Behavior: Researching the Brain

A Global Vista: Cross-Cultural Research

How to Evaluate a Study Critically

One Step Further: Ethical Questions Come in Shades of Gray

Central Questions: How Do We Know When We Know Something?

LEARNING OBJECTIVES

Upon completion of Chapter 2, you should be able to answer the following questions.

1.   What are the four characteristics of good psychological research?

2.   What are a theory, a hypothesis, and a variable?

3.   Differentiate between the internal and external validity of a study.

4.   What is meant by the *reliability* of a measure? Discuss three important kinds of reliability.

5.   How do researchers ensure the *validity* of a psychological measure?

6.   Why are multiple measures important to obtain an accurate assessment of a variable?

7.   How do experimental methods allow researchers to assess cause-and-effect relations between variables?

8. How do independent and dependent variables differ?

9. What are the six steps involved in conceiving and executing an experiment?

10. Why are control groups important in experimental research?

11. What is the purpose of blind studies in experimental research? How do double-blind studies differ from single-blind studies?

12. Why is random assignment important in experimental research?

13. What are two limitations of experimental research?

14. What is a quasi-experimental design and why do researchers use such designs?

15. What are the advantages and limitations of each of the following descriptive methods?

    Case study

    Naturalistic observation

    Survey research

16. How do researchers using the survey method ensure that their sample reflects the demographic characteristics of the population of interest?

17. How do correlation coefficients represent the relation between variables? What is the difference between positive and negative correlations?

18. What is meant by the phrase "correlation does not imply causation"?

19. Compare the following methods researchers use to study the brain:

   electroencephalogram (EEG)

   computerized axial tomography (CT-scan)

   magnetic resonance imaging (MRI)

   positron emission tomography (PET)

   functional magnetic resonance imaging (fMRI).

20. What difficulties do researchers face when trying to transport research from one culture to another?

21. What are seven important criteria that can be used to evaluate a study critically?

22. What four conditions must be met before deception can be used in a study?

23. Discuss the ethical controversy concerning the use of animals in psychological research.

PART TWO: REVIEW AND LEARN
Key Terms, Fill-In Exercises, Application and Using What You Have Learned

Before doing the exercises below, review the information you learned in this chapter. Reread the work you did in part one of this study guide chapter, plus the interim summaries and end-of-chapter summary in your textbook. Review any problem areas. Once you feel comfortable with the material, do the following exercises without referring to your notes or textbook. If you have difficulty with a term or question, mark it and come back to it. When you have finished an exercise, go back to your notes and the textbook to find the answers to the questions that gave you difficulty. Finally, check your answers (key terms against the textbook and the rest against the answer key).

KEY TERMS

Theory _____

_____

Hypothesis _____

_____

Variable _____

_____

Continuous variable _____

_____

Categorical variable _____

_____

Standardized procedures _____

_____

Population _____

_____

Sample   _____

_____

Representative _____

_____

Participants (or Subjects)   _____

_____

Generalizability _____

_____

Valid   _____

_____

Internal validity _____

_____

External validity _____

_____

Measure   _____

_____

Reliability   _____

_____

Retest reliability _____

_____

Internal consistency   _____

_____

Interrater reliability _____

_____

Validity _____

_____

Validation _____

_____

Error _____

_____

Experimental research _____

_____

Independent variable _____

_____

Dependent variable _____

_____

Conditions _____

_____

Operationalizing_____

_____

Control group _____

_____

Demand characteristics _____

_____

Blind studies _____

_____

Placebo effect _____

_____

Single-blind study _____

_____

Double-blind study _____

_____

Confounding variable _____

_____

Descriptive statistics _____

_____

Inferential statistics _____

_____

Quasi-experimental designs _____

_____

Descriptive research _____

_____

Case study _____

_____

Naturalistic observation _____

_____

Survey research _____

_____

Interviews _____

_____

Questionnaires _____

_____

Random sample _____

_____

Stratified random sample _____

_____

Correlational research _____

_____

Correlate _____

_____

Correlation coefficient _____

_____

Positive correlation _____

_____

Negative correlation _____

_____

Correlation matrix _____

_____

Electroencephalogram (EEG)   _____

_____

Neuroimaging techniques   _____

_____

Computerized axial tomography (CT-scan or CAT-scan)   _____

_____

Magnetic resonance imaging (MRI)   _____

_____

Positron emission tomography (PET)   _____

_____

Functional magnetic resonance imaging (fMRI)   _____

_____

FILL-IN EXERCISES

Fill in the word or words that best fit in the spaces below.

1.   The individuals who take part in a study are referred to as _____.

2.   A variable that can be placed on a continuum is a _____ variable, whereas one comprised of groupings or categories is a _____ variable.

3.   Researchers typically study the behavior of a particular subset of people in order to learn about the larger _____.

4.   The term _____ refers to a measure's ability to produce consistent results.

5.   The ability of a measure to assess the variable it is supposed to measure is referred to as its _____.

6.   Because every measure includes some degree of error, investigators often employ _____ measures of the variable.

7.   Using experimental methods allows researchers to directly assess _____-and-_____ relations between variables.

8.   Turning an abstract concept into a concrete variable is called _____ the variable.

9.   To ensure that the only things that vary from participant to participant are the independent variables and the participants' performance on the dependent variables, investigators develop a _____ procedure for all participants.

10.   A _____-_____ study is a way of reducing the effects of the biases of both participants and researchers .

11.   In analyzing the findings of a study, _____ statistics are used to summarize the essential features of the data, whereas _____ statistics are used to draw inferences from the sample studied to the population as a whole.

12.   Psychologists who take an *interpretive* (or *hermeneutic*) approach to methodology often use _____ studies; their aim is to examine the complex meanings that may underlie human behavior.

13.   An advantage of experiments is that they can be _____, that is, repeated to see if the same findings emerge with a different sample.

14.   The two most frequently used tools of survey researchers are _____ and _____.

15.   When using survey methods, sometimes proportional representation of different subpopulations is important to researchers. A _____ random sample specifies the percentage of participants to be drawn from each population category and then _____ selects from within each category.

USING WHAT YOU HAVE LEARNED

In Chapter 2, you learned about different research methods that are used in psychology. Below you will find the names of various research methods. Identify which method best describes each of the examples of research studies that follow.

Research Methods

Naturalistic observation
Survey research
Quasi-experiment

Case study
Correlational research
Experiment

Studies

1. The relation between college students' final exam grades and the number of hours they spent studying for the exam is examined.

2. A psychology professor wants to determine whether showing videotapes as an adjunct to his lectures improves students' performance. He randomly creates two groups of students: those in one group watch videotapes that illustrate the material in the lecture, while those in the other just attend the lectures (no tapes). He then compares their grades on the exam.

3. A researcher is interested in whether there are sex differences in grades in the Introduction to psychology course. She compares the grades of the female students to those of the male students in the course.

4. Every term, the university asks students to complete a questionnaire evaluating the course they are taking and the professor who teaches it. The information is used to provide feedback to the department and to the professors concerning both course content and teaching methods.

5. A team of developmental psychologists, interested in the phenomenon of bullying, spends several weeks observing children at recess and lunch break in their school playground.

6. A clinical psychologist collects considerable information concerning each patient that she sees, including information concerning their childhood (family and school experiences), job and career, romantic relationships, and so on. Her goal is to put together a comprehensive picture of each patient.

APPLICATION

Situation

A researcher is interested in whether taking vitamin C has an effect on the number of colds people get.

Questions to Answer

1. If she wants to determine whether taking vitamin C actually reduces the number of colds people get (i.e., a cause-and-effect relationship), what type of research procedure should she use?

2. What procedures would she follow in setting up such a study?

3. What could she select for the independent and dependent variables?

4. Do you think a control group would be important? Why? What kind of neutral condition could she use with a control group?

5. How could she control for possible demand characteristics in the study?

PART THREE: TEST AND KNOW
SAMPLE TEST QUESTIONS

Test how well you have learned this chapter's material by answering the sample test questions. You may wish to mark your answers on a separate sheet of paper so you can reuse this test for exam review. Once you have completed the exam, check your answers and then go back to your notes and the textbook to review questions you found difficult.

1. Because case study research gains its insights from examining only one participant, generalization to a larger population is always uncertain. One way to minimize this limitation is to

   a. use a multiple case study approach
   b. avoid using the case study
   c. employ experimental case study designs
   d. stop trying to generalize

2. The term _____ refers to the applicability of a study's findings to the entire population of interest to the researchers.

   a. internal validity   b. generalizability
   c. reliability   d. internal consistency

3.   A researcher is interested in whether watching "Sesame Street" on TV has a positive impact on children's grades at school. She records the number of days children watch "Sesame Street" over a one-month interval and relates it to their grades on their report cards at school. This study is best described as

    a.   experimental
    b.   quasi-experimental
    c.   a survey
    d.   correlational

4.   Operationalizing the variable involves

    a.   turning an abstract concept into a concrete variable
    b.   predicting the relation between two or more variables
    c.   putting your research plan into operation
    d.   manipulating a variable and observing the operation of its effects

5.   The major problem with survey methods is the following:

    a.   It is often difficult to get participants to participate in this kind of study.
    b.   They rely on participants to report on themselves truthfully and accurately.
    c.   It is questionable whether the results can be generalized to the larger population.
    d.   It is often difficult to keep participants unaware of the purpose of the study and thus demand characteristics can be a major concern.

6.   In an experiment, the investigator can determine whether a _____ relation exists between two variables, whereas this cannot be determined in a study using correlational methods.

    a.   valid
    b.   cause-and-effect
    c.   generalizable
    d   reliable

7.   Assume an investigator has found a positive correlation between the number of aspirins people take and the number of headaches they get. The investigator could conclude the following from this correlation:

    a.   The number of aspirins taken and number of headaches suffered are related to one another.
    b.   People who take aspirin frequently seem to get fewer headaches.
    c.   Taking aspirin causes people to have fewer headaches.
    d.   Taking aspirin seems unrelated to whether people have headaches or not.

8.   A hypothetical study of the relation between TV violence and aggressive behavior in children reveals a correlation of +.85 between the number of violent shows watched each week and children's level of aggressiveness. Based on these findings, which of the following conclusions might be true?

    a.   Watching violent TV leads to aggressive behavior in children.
    b.   Parents who do not allow their children to watch violent shows may discourage aggressive behavior in their children in other ways as well.
    c.   Children who are more aggressive may have more of a "taste" for violent shows than those who are less aggressive.
    d.   In fact, ALL of the above conclusions could be true.

9.   A researcher has developed a new treatment for smoking which combines hypnosis and acupuncture. He randomly creates two groups of participants and administers his new treatment to one group, while the other group receives no treatment. He measures the number of cigarettes participants smoke in the two weeks following treatment. This study is best described as

    a.   descriptive   b.   correlational
    c.   quasi-experimental   d.   experimental

10.   What is the dependent variable in the previous example?

    a.   the two groups of participants   b.   the 2 weeks following treatment
    c.   hypnosis and acupuncture   d.   the number of cigarettes smoked

11.   In the previous example, it would be important for the researchers to ensure that participants are kept unaware of the goals of the research; otherwise, their behavior might be affected. To do so, the researcher would conduct

    a.   a single-blind study   b.   a. quasi-experimental study
    c.   a case study   d.   a demand characteristic

12.   In the previous example, if participants in the treatment condition were older than those in the no-treatment condition, _____ would be a confounding variable.

    a.   smoking   b.   the treatment
    c.   age   d.   no treatment

13.   A correlation of zero means that

    a.   two variables are unrelated
    b.   as the first variable increases, the other decreases
    c.   as the first variable decreases, the other increases
    d.   participants tended to score around zero on both variables

14.   A procedure in which radioactive glucose is injected into the bloodstream allowing researchers to observe the brain in action is called

        a.   an electroencephalogram (EEG)
        b.   computerized axial tomography (CT scan)
        c.   magnetic resonance imaging (MRI)
        d.   positron emission tomography (PET)

15.   When deception is used in research, researchers must be sure to

        a.   pay the participants
        b.   debrief the participants afterward
        c.   instruct the participants not to talk about the true purposes of the study
        d.   ensure that participants do not deduce the true purpose of the study, which could cause demand characteristics to bias the results

16.   Experimental and quasi-experimental designs are useful in the context of _____, whereas case studies, naturalistic observation, and correlational studies are often more useful in the context of _____.

        a.   justification; discovery   b.   discovery; justification
        c.   reliability; validation   d.   validation; reliability

17.   A systematic way to organize and explain observations, which includes a set of propositions or statements about the relations among various phenomena is a

        a.   hypothesis   b.   paradigm
        c.   theory   d.   model

18.   If several ways of asking the same question yield similar results, a measure has

        a.   retest reliability   b.   internal consistency
        c.   interrater reliability   d.   internal validity

19.   If the finding of a study can be generalized to situations outside the laboratory, the study has

        a.   internal validity   b.   internal consistency
        c.   external consistency   d.   external validity

20.   The number that indicates the direction and strength of the relation between two variables is referred to as a

        a.   correlation coefficient   b.   correlation matrix
        c.   scatter plot   d.   correlation plot

ANSWERS

FILL-IN EXERCISES

1. participants (or subjects) 2. continuous; categorical 3. population 4. reliability 5. validity 6. multiple 7. cause; effect 8. operationalizing 9. standardized 10. double-blind 11. descriptive; inferential 12. case 13. replicated 14. questionnaires; interviews 15. stratified; randomly

APPLICATION

1. Experimental research
2. Follow the six steps of conceiving and executing an experiment: frame hypothesis; operationalize variables; develop standardized procedures; select and assign participants to conditions; apply statistical techniques to the results; and draw conclusions.
3. Independent variable -- level of vitamin C administered to each group (e.g., 0 mg/day; 100 mg/day; 500 mg/day); Dependent variable -- number of colds participants in each group report during the duration of the study.
4. Yes; because of placebo effects. Use a placebo control (e.g., an inert pill).
5. Use a blind study (single-blind to control for demand characteristics; double blind to control as well for experimenter bias).

USING WHAT YOU HAVE LEARNED

1. correlational research 2. experiment 3. quasi-experiment 4. survey research
5. naturalistic observation 6. case study

SAMPLE TEST QUESTIONS

1.	a	11.	a
2.	b	12.	c
3.	d	13.	a
4.	a	14.	d
5.	b	15.	b
6.	b	16.	a
7.	a	17.	c
8.	d	18.	b
9.	d	19.	d
10.	d	20.	a

Chapter 2:Supplement
Statistical Principles
in Psychological Research

PART ONE: PRE-READ AND WORK
Outline and Learning Objectives

Pre-read this chapter's table of contents and end-of-chapter summary. Then, use the outline segment-by-segment to help you work through the chapter. Jot down your own questions, comments, and notes in the space provided. Make a note of difficult areas that you will need to review (include page numbers). Then, answer the questions in the learning objectives section that follows. Check off those you are confident that you can answer well. Re-read the material in the text for the questions about which you are less confident. Record the important points from your reading in the space below each question.

OUTLINE

Summarizing the Data: Descriptive Statistics

Measures of Central Tendency

Variability

The Normal Distribution

Testing the Hypothesis: Inferential Statistics

Statistical Significance

Common Tests of Statistical Significance

Central Questions: What Does It Mean to Say That A Finding is "Significant"?

LEARNING OBJECTIVES

Upon completion of Chapter 2: Supplement, you should be able to answer the following questions..

1.   How do researchers chart a frequency distribution?

2.   What are the similarities and differences between the three most common measures of central tendency -- mean, mode, and median?

3.   What are two methods of measuring variability?

4.   What are the important characteristics of a normal distribution?

5.   Why are tests of statistical significance necessary?

6.   What is meant by the expression "$p < .01$?"

7.   What are two frequently used tests of statistical significance? When would it be appropriate to use one or the other?

8.   What are some issues concerning the notion of the "significance" of findings?

PART TWO: REVIEW AND LEARN
Key Terms, Fill-In Exercises, Application and Using What You Have Learned

Before doing the exercises below, review the information you learned in this chapter. Reread the work you did in part one of this study guide chapter, plus the interim summaries and end-of-chapter summary in your textbook. Review any problem areas. Once you feel comfortable with the material, do the following exercises without referring to your notes or textbook. If you have difficulty with a term or question, mark it and come back to it. When you have finished an exercise, go back to your notes and the textbook to find the answers to the questions that gave you difficulty. Finally, check your answers (key terms against the textbook and the rest against the answer key).

KEY TERMS

Upon completion of Chapter 2: Supplement, you should be able to define the following terms.

Descriptive Statistics   _____

_____

Inferential Statistics   _____

_____

Frequency distribution   _____

_____

Histogram   _____

_____

Measures of central tendency   _____

_____

Mean _____

_____

Mode _____

_____

Median _____

_____

Variability _____

_____

Range _____

_____

Standard deviation (SD) _____

_____

Normal distribution _____

_____

Percentile Scores _____

_____

Statistical significance _____

_____

Probability value (*p*-value) _____

_____

Chi-square test (or χ^2) _____

_____

t-test   _____

_____

Analysis of variance (ANOVA)   _____

_____

APPLICATION

Situation

A researcher is interested in whether there is a significant difference between science students and general arts students in amount of time spent studying. She administers a questionnaire that asks the number of hours spent studying over the past week to 15 science students and 15 general arts students. She collects the following results:

Science Students		General Arts Students	
Student #	Studying Hours	Student #	Studying Hours
1	20	1	19
2	20	2	27
3	28	3	32
4	21	4	23
5	28	5	27
6	21	6	31
7	35	7	27
8	30	8	16
9	28	9	17
10	22	10	25
11	25	11	26
12	26	12	28
13	19	13	22
14	27	14	29
15	24	15	24

Questions to Answer

1.   Calculate the mean, median, and mode for each group of students.

2.   Calculate the range of scores for each group.

3.   What would be the appropriate test to assess whether there is a statistically significant difference between the two groups? What would be an acceptable *p* value for the difference?

FILL-IN EXERCISES

Fill in the word or words that best fit in the spaces below.

1.   A method of organizing the data to show how frequently subjects received each of the many possible scores is referred to as a _____ _____.

2.   The three most common measures of central tendency are the _____, the _____, and the _____.

3.   The simplest measure of variability is the _____ of scores.

4.   A _____-value represents the probability that the results obtained in a study were just a matter of chance.

5.   If both the independent and dependent variables are categorical, the appropriate statistic is a(n) _____.

PART THREE: TEST AND KNOW
SAMPLE TEST QUESTIONS

Test how well you have learned this chapter's material by answering the sample test questions. You may wish to mark your answers on a separate sheet of paper so you can reuse this test for exam review. Once you have completed the exam, check your answers and then go back to your notes and the textbook to review questions you found difficult.

1.   The score that falls in the middle of a distribution of scores, with half the subjects scoring below it and half above it, is the

a.	mean	b.	mode
c.	median	d.	standard deviation

2.   A frequency distribution in which the ranges of scores are plotted along the X-axis and the frequency of scores in each range is plotted on the Y-axis is referred to as a

a.	measure of central tendency	b.	bell-curve
c.	normal distribution	d.	histogram

3.   A measure of variability that is more useful than the *range* is the

a.	histogram	b.	normal distribution
c.	central tendency	d.	standard deviation

4.   In a(n) _____ _____, the scores of most subjects fall in the middle of the bell-shaped distribution, and progressively fewer subjects have scores at either extreme.

   a.   normal distribution   b.   standard deviation
   c.   inferential statistic   d.   frequency distribution

5.   Tests of statistical significance determine

   a.   whether the results of a study are high in practical significance
   b.   whether the results of a study are high in theoretical significance
   c.   whether the results of a study are likely to have occurred simply by chance
   d.   whether the results of a study apply to situations outside the lab in which the research took place

6.   By convention, psychologists accept the results of a study whenever the probability of findings attributable to chance is less than

   a.   50%   b.   10%
   c.   5%   d.   1%

7.   The best way to ensure that the results of a study are not accidental is to

   a.   use a frequency distribution   b.   use a large sample of subjects.
   c.   use a normal distribution.   d.   use a chi-square test.

8.   If the independent variable is categorical, while the dependent variable is continuous, the most appropriate test of statistical significance would be a(n)

   a.   analysis of variance   b.   chi-squared test
   c.   standard deviation   d.   correlation

9.   The expression p<.01 means

   a.   the chances of the findings of this study being spurious are 1 in 100
   b.   there is a good chance that less than 100 subjects participated in this study
   c.   only 1 out of a sample of 100 likely participated in this study
   d.   the results of this study apply only to 1 in 100 individuals

10.   The statistical test that compares observed data with the results that would be expected by chance and tests the likelihood that the differences between observed and expected are accidental is a(n)

   a.   analysis of variance   b.   chi-squared test.
   c.   t-test.   d.   a correlation

ANSWERS

FILL-IN EXERCISES

1. frequency distribution 2. mean, median, mode 3. range 4. p (or probability)
5. chi-square test (or χ^2)

APPLICATION

1.		Science Students	Arts Students
	mean	24.93	24.87
	median	25	26
	mode	28	27
2.	range	16	16

3.   t-test; $p<.05$

SAMPLE TEST QUESTIONS

1.   c
2.   d
3.   d
4.   a
5.   c
6.   c
7.   b
8.   a
9.   a
10.   b

Chapter 3
Biological Bases
of Mental Life and Behavior

PART ONE: PRE-READ AND WORK
Outline and Learning Objectives

Pre-read this chapter's table of contents and end-of-chapter summary. Then, use the outline segment-by-segment to help you work through the chapter. Jot down your own questions, comments, and notes in the space provided. Make a note of key terms and of difficult areas that you will need to review (include page numbers). Then, answer the questions in the learning objectives section that follows. Check off those you are confident that you can answer well. Re-read the material in the text for the questions about which you are less confident. Record the important points from your reading in the space below each question.

OUTLINE

Neurons: Basic Units of the Nervous System

Anatomy of a Neuron

Firing of a Neuron

Transmission of Information Between Cells

The Endocrine System

The Peripheral Nervous System

The Somatic Nervous System

The Autonomic Nervous System

The Central Nervous System

Evolution of the Central Nervous System

The Spinal Cord

The Hindbrain

The Midbrain

The Forebrain

The Cerebral Cortex

From Brain to Behavior: The Impact of Frontal Lobe Damage on Personality

A Global Vista: Environment, Culture, and the Brain

Brain, Gene, and Behavior

Genetics

Behavioral Genetics

Central Questions: Brain-Behavior Relationships

LEARNING OBJECTIVES

Upon completion of Chapter 3, you should be able to answer the following questions.

1.   What are three kinds of neurons and what are their functions?

2.   What are the functions of the dendrites, the cell body, and the axon?

3.   Why is myelination important for the transmission of nerve impulses?

4.   How do graded potentials differ from action potentials?

5.   How are sodium and potassium ions involved in the transmission of an impulse down the axon?

6.   How do neurons communicate chemically with other neurons?

7.   How do excitatory and inhibitory neurotransmitters differ?

8.   What are the psychological functions of the following neurotransmitters?

Glutamate

GABA (Gamma-aminobutyric acid)

Dopamine

Serotonin

Acetylcholine (Ach)

Endorphins

9.   What is Parkinson's disease and what role does dopamine play in this disease?

10.   What are the functions of the following endocrine glands?

Pituitary gland

Thyroid gland

Adrenal glands

Gonads

11.   In what ways do the functions of the sympathetic nervous system and the parasympathetic nervous system differ?

12.   What is the major function of each of the following areas of the hindbrain?

Medulla oblongata

Cerebellum

Reticular formation

13.   What are the major functions of the areas of the midbrain called the tectum and tegmentum?

14.   What is the major function of each of the following areas of the forebrain?

Hypothalamus

Thalamus

Limbic System

Basal ganglia

15.   What are three functions performed by the cerebral cortex?

16.   What are the major functions of each of the following four lobes of the cerebral cortex?

Occipital

Parietal

Frontal

Temporal

17.   How do the functions of the primary and association areas of the cortex differ?

18.   How is space allocated to different parts of the body in the motor and somatosensory cortexes?

19.   What are the results of damage to Broca's and Wernicke's areas?

20.   Describe the personality changes that are consequences of damage to the frontal lobes.

21.   What is meant by cerebral lateralization? List the various functions for which the left and right hemisphere are dominant.

22.   How does split-brain research provide evidence for cerebral lateralization?

23.   What cognitive and/or motor differences have been found between females and males? What are the biological and cultural explanations for these differences?

24.   How are the genes from each parent transmitted to their children?

25.   How do researchers assess the heritability of various characteristics?

PART TWO: REVIEW AND LEARN
Key Terms, Fill-In Exercises, Application and Using What You Have Learned

Before doing the exercises below, review the information you learned in this chapter. Reread the work you did in part one of this study guide chapter, plus the interim summaries and end-of-chapter summary in your textbook. Review any problem areas. Once you feel comfortable with the material, do the following exercises without referring to your notes or textbook. If you have difficulty with a term or question, mark it and come back to it. When you have finished an exercise, go back to your notes and the textbook to find the answers to the questions that gave you difficulty. Finally, check your answers (key terms against the textbook and the rest against the answer key).

KEY TERMS

Nervous system _____

_____

Neurons   _____

_____

Sensory neurons   _____

_____

Interneurons   _____

_____

Motor neurons   _____

_____

Dendrites   _____

_____

Cell body   _____

_____

Axon _____

_____

Myelin sheath _____

_____

Terminal buttons _____

_____

Synapses_____

_____

Resting potential _____

_____

Graded potentials _____

_____

Action potentials _____

_____

Neurotransmitters _____

_____

Receptors _____

_____

Glutamate _____

_____

GABA _____

_____

Dopamine   _____

_____

Parkinson's disease   _____

_____

Serotonin   _____

_____

Acetylcholine (Ach)   _____

_____

Endorphins   _____

_____

Endocrine system   _____

_____

Hormones   _____

_____

Adrenaline and noradrenaline   _____

_____

Pituitary gland   _____

_____

Thyroid gland   _____

_____

Adrenal glands   _____

_____

Gonads _____

_____

Testosterone _____

_____

Estrogens _____

_____

Central nervous system (CNS) _____

_____

Peripheral nervous system (PNS) _____

_____

Somatic nervous system _____

_____

Autonomic nervous system (ANS) _____

_____

Sympathetic nervous system _____

_____

Parasympathetic nervous system _____

_____

Spinal cord _____

_____

Hindbrain _____

_____

Medulla oblongata   _____

_____

Cerebellum   _____

_____

Reticular formation   _____

_____

Midbrain   _____

_____

Tectum _____

_____

Tegmentum   _____

_____

Forebrain   _____

_____

Hypothalamus _____

_____

Thalamus   _____

_____

Limbic system   _____

_____

Amygdala   _____

_____

Hippocampus _____

_____

Basal ganglia _____

_____

Cerebral cortex _____

_____

Primary areas _____

_____

Association areas _____

_____

Cerebral hemispheres _____

_____

Corpus callosum _____

_____

Occipital lobes _____

_____

Parietal lobes _____

_____

Somatosensory cortex _____

_____

Frontal lobes _____

_____

Motor cortex _____

_____

Broca's area _____

_____

Temporal lobes _____

_____

Wernicke's area _____

_____

Cerebral lateralization _____

_____

Split-brain patient _____

_____

Gene _____

_____

Chromosomes _____

_____

Degree of relatedness _____

_____

Monozygotic (MZ) twins _____

_____

Dizygotic (DZ) twins _____

_____

Heritability coefficient   _____

_____

Heritability   _____

_____

FILL-IN EXERCISES

Fill in the word or words that best fit in the spaces below.

1.   _____ neurons transmit information from receptors to the brain. _____ neurons transmit commands from interneurons to the glands and muscles of the body.

2.   Branch-like extensions of the neuron, called _____, receive inputs from other neurons. If a neuron receives enough stimulation, it passes information to other neurons through its _____.

3.   The _____ matter of the brain is composed of myelinated _____.

4.   Multiple sclerosis is a disease in which the _____ sheath on large clusters of neurons degenerates, causing jerky, uncoordinated movement.

5.   An _____ (*increase/decrease*) in polarization inhibits the neuron, making it less likely to fire.

6.   _____ are chemicals that transmit information from one cell to another.

7.   Glutamate is a neurotransmitter that can _____ (*excite/inhibit*) nearly every neuron in the nervous system, whereas GABA is a neurotransmitter that plays an _____ (*excitatory/inhibitory*) role.

8.   The neurotransmitter _____ is involved in learning and memory.

9.   The hormone adrenaline is the same compound as the neurotransmitter _____.

10.   The _____ gland is often described as the *"master gland"* because many of the hormones it releases stimulate and regulate the other glands.

11.   The _____ gland releases hormones that control growth and metabolism.

12.   The male gonads, referred to as _____, produce the hormone _____. The female gonads, referred to as _____, produce the hormone _____.

13.   The somatic nervous system, because it is involved in intentional actions, is sometimes also called the _____ nervous system.

14. The _____ _____ sends information from sensory neurons in various parts of the body to the brain, and it relays motor commands back to muscles and organs..

15. The _____ is the area of the hindbrain involved in coordinating smooth, well-sequenced movements, and in maintaining balance and posture.

16. Damage to the _____ _____ is a major cause of coma.

17. The _____ _____ is a set of structures in the forebrain with diverse functions involving emotion, motivation, learning, and memory.

18. The hills and valleys making up the convolutions of the cortex are referred to as _____ and _____, respectively.

19. The _____ areas of the cortex process raw sensory information or initiate motor movements, while the _____ areas are involved in constructing perceptions, ideas, and plans.

20. The _____ lobes are involved in the sense of touch, detecting movement in the environment, locating objects in space, and experiencing one's own body as it moves through space.

21. The _____ lobes are particularly important in audition and language.

22. In general, the _____ hemisphere tends to be dominant for language, logic, complex motor behavior, and aspects of consciousness (particularly verbal aspects), whereas the _____ tends to be dominant for nonlinguistic functions.

23. _____ twins develop from the union of the same sperm and egg. Their degree of relatedness is _____.

APPLICATION

In each of the following hypothetical examples, an individual has suffered an injury to some area of the brain. Try to determine, from what you've read in Chapter 3, where the injury may be.

1. Following neurosurgery to control life-threatening seizures, a patient is unable to remember new information. You have interviewed this patient on several occasions, yet every time you meet with her, she introduces herself anew to you.

2. Following a car accident in which her head violently struck the dashboard, a patient reports difficulty motivating herself and cannot seem to get started on any task. She has become quiet and withdrawn, preferring to spend her time alone, doing nothing.

3. Following a stroke, a patient has difficulty understanding words and sentences spoken by others. She does attempt to speak, and her speech has normal rhythm and fluency; however, it makes little sense – it's a "word salad."

USING WHAT YOU HAVE LEARNED

In Chapter 3, the sympathetic nervous system was described as an emergency system that is activated in response to threats. Its job is to ready the body for fight or flight, and it does so in several ways. Anxiety and panic attacks were described as the result of such sympathetic activity, where the autonomic nervous system may over-react to an event in the environment. Think back to a situation in which you recently experienced anxiety. It may have been a situation where you had to speak before a group of people. Maybe it involved writing an examination. Or maybe it was flying or riding in a fast moving elevator.

1.   What kind of physical sensations did you experience?

2.   Can you see how those sensations reflect the functioning of the sympathetic nervous system?

3.   Can you see the potentially adaptive role those sensations might have, had you been experiencing real physical threat?

4.   Think of the role the adrenal glands play in such a situation. Can you remember feeling aroused and jittery for some time even after the event had passed because of the higher levels of adrenaline in your blood?

PART THREE: TEST AND KNOW
SAMPLE TEST QUESTIONS

Test how well you have learned this chapter's material by answering the sample test questions. You may wish to mark your answers on a separate sheet of paper so you can reuse this test for exam review. Once you have completed the exam, check your answers and then go back to your notes and the textbook to review questions you found difficult.

1.   The nervous system is comprised of three types of neurons:

    a.   sensory neurons, motor neurons, and interneurons
    b.   sensory neurons, spinal neurons, and interneurons
    c.   myelinated axons, dendrites, and unmyelinated axons and dendrites
    d.   sensory neurons, motor neurons, and efferent neurons

2.   The "gray matter" of the brain gets its color from

    a.   myelinated axons
    b.   cell bodies, dendrites, and unmyelinated axons
    c.   synapses
    d.   myelinated cell bodies and dendrites

3.   Connections between neurons occur at what are called

    a.   terminal buttons
    b.   nodes of Ranvier
    c.   receptors
    d.   synapses

4.   Unlike a graded potential, _____ has an *"all-or-none"* quality.

    a.   an action potential
    b.   a resting potential
    c.   depolarization
    d.   hyperpolarization

5.   Some people respond to MSG in Chinese food with neurological symptoms such as tingling and numbing, because the ingredient activates _____ receptors in their brains.

    a.   GABA
    b.   glutamate
    c.   dopamine
    d.   acetylcholine

6.   The neurotransmitter involved in the regulation of mood, sleep, eating, emotional arousal, and pain regulation is

    a.   dopamine
    b.   serotonin
    c.   acetylcholine
    d.   endorphin

7.   Parkinson's disease results from degeneration of the _____-releasing cells of the substantia nigra.

    a.   acetylcholine
    b.   serotonin
    c.   dopamine
    d.   endorphin

8.   The endocrine gland(s) that is (are) more directly connected to the CNS than any other endocrine gland is (are) the

    a.   thyroid gland
    b.   adrenal glands
    c.   pituitary gland
    d.   gonads

9.   The nervous system that prepares the body for fighting or fleeing in response to threats is the

    a.   sympathetic nervous system
    b.   parasympathetic nervous system
    c.   somatic nervous system
    d.   peripheral nervous system

10.   Sexual activity is a good example of how the _____ and _____ nervous systems interact

    a.   central; peripheral
    b.   somatic; autonomic
    c.   afferent; efferent
    d.   sympathetic; parasympathetic

11.   The area of the hindbrain responsible for maintaining consciousness, regulating arousal levels, and modulating the activity of neurons throughout the central nervous system is the

    a.   medulla oblongata
    b.   cerebellum
    c.   reticular formation
    d.   thalamus

12.   One of the most important functions of the hypothalamus is

    a.   relaying sensory information to higher brain centers
    b.   maintaining consciousness and regulating activity states
    c.   homeostasis
    d.   coordinating smooth, well-sequenced movements

13.   The structure within the limbic system that is especially involved in learning and remembering emotionally significant events is the

    a.   amygdala
    b.   hippocampus
    c.   septal area
    d.   basal ganglia

14.   The occipital lobes of the cerebral cortex are involved in

    a.   the sense of touch and the experience of one's own body in space.
    b.   visual sensation and perception.
    c.   attention, planning, abstract thinking, and social skills.
    d.   auditory sensation and perception and language.

15. A brain-injured patient appears callous, grandiose, and boastful, and tends to make tactless comments. The area of the brain that is most likely damaged is the

    a.   frontal lobes
    b.   parietal lobes
    c.   occipital lobes
    d.   temporal lobes

16. In most people, the right hemisphere is dominant for

    a.   language
    b.   logic
    c.   analytical thinking
    d.   recognition of faces and places

17. On the average, males score higher than females on tests of

    a.   manual dexterity
    b.   verbal fluency
    c.   perceptual speed
    d.   spatial processing

18. Psychologists interested in genetics study the influence of genetic blueprints, referred to as _____, on observable psychological attributes or qualities, referred to as _____.

    a.   chromosomes; genes
    b.   phenotypes; genotypes
    c.   genotypes; phenotypes
    d.   heritability coefficients; degree of relatedness

19. Which type of twins share as much with each other, in terms of degree of relatedness, as they do with each of their parents?

    a.   monozygotic twins
    b.   dizygotic twins
    c.   trizygotic twins
    d.   identical twins

20. The term "heritability" refers to

    a.   genetic influences on variability among individuals
    b.   the extent to which a trait is genetically determined
    c.   the degree to which various relatives share genetic material
    d.   the degree to which MZ twins and DZ twins differ on a particular trait

ANSWERS

FILL-IN EXERCISES

1. sensory (or afferent); motor (or efferent)   2. dendrites; axon   3. white; axons   4. myelin
5. increase   6. neurotransmitters   7. excite; inhibitory   8. acetylcholine (ACh)   9. epinephrine
10. pituitary 11. thyroid 12. testes, testosterone; ovaries, estrogen 13. voluntary   14. spinal cord
15. cerebellum 16. reticular formation   17. limbic system   18. gyri; sulci   19. primary; association
20. parietal   21. temporal 22. left; right   23. monozygotic; 1.0

APPLICATION

1. hippocampus 2. frontal lobes 3. Wernicke's area

SAMPLE TEST QUESTIONS

1.	a	11.	c
2.	b	12.	c
3.	d	13.	a
4.	a	14.	b
5.	b	15.	a
6.	b	16.	d
7.	c	17.	d
8.	c	18.	c
9.	a	19.	b
10.	d	20.	a

Chapter 4
Sensation and Perception

PART ONE: PRE-READ AND WORK
Outline and Learning Objectives

Pre-read this chapter's table of contents and end-of-chapter summary. Then, use the outline segment-by-segment to help you work through the chapter. Jot down your own questions, comments, and notes in the space provided. Make a note of key terms and of difficult areas that you will need to review (include page numbers). Then, answer the questions in the learning objectives section that follows. Check off those you are confident that you can answer well. Re-read the material in the text for the questions about which you are less confident. Record the important points from your reading in the space below each question.

OUTLINE

Basic Principles

Sensing the Environment

Transduction

Absolute Thresholds

One Step Further: Signal Detection

Difference Thresholds

Sensory Adaptation

Vision

The Nature of Light

The Eye

Neural Pathways

Perceiving in Color

Hearing

The Nature of Sound

The Ear

Neural Pathways

Other Senses

Smell

Taste

Skin Senses

From Brain to Behavior: Personality and Pain

Proprioceptive Senses

Perception

Organizing Sensory Experience

A Global Vista: Culture and Perceptual Illusions

Interpreting Sensory Experience

Central Questions: Physical Reality and Psychological Reality

LEARNING OBJECTIVES

Upon completion of Chapter 4, you should be able to answer the following questions.

1.   How does perception differ from sensation?

2.   What three general principles underlie the processes of sensation and perception?

3.   Discuss the following five features that are common to all sensory modalities:

Transduction

Absolute thresholds

Signal detection

Difference threshold

Sensory adaptation

4.   What is Weber's law? Fechner's law? Stevens' power law? What are the strengths and weaknesses of each?

5.   Describe the path light travels as it enters the eye and is focused on the retina.

6.   How do photoreceptors transform light into sight?

7.   Describe the neural pathway followed by impulses from the optic nerve to the visual cortex.

8.   What is the trichromatic theory of color?

9.   What is the opponent-process theory of color, and how does it explain afterimages and color blindness?

10. What is the difference between the acoustic energy properties of frequency, complexity, and amplitude?

11. What are the roles of the outer, middle, and inner ear in the process of hearing?

12. How do place theory and frequency theory explain the experiences of pitch and loudness?

13. Describe the neural pathway followed by impulses from the auditory nerve to the auditory cortex.

14. How do humans localize sound?

15. Describe the path to the brain followed by information from the smell receptors and taste receptors.

16. What is meant by the term *phantom limbs*?

17. What are the three qualities that constitute the sense of touch?

18. Explain the gate-control theory of pain.

19.   Are chronic pain and personality style related?

20.   Describe two proprioceptive senses -- kinesthesia and the vestibular sense.

21.   Distinguish among the following four aspects of perceptual organization: form perception, depth perception, movement perception, and perceptual constancy.

22.   What are the six basic perceptual rules, according to Gestalt psychologists, that the brain follows as it organizes sensory input into meaningful wholes?

23.   What is Biederman's *recognition-by-components* theory? How would it explain channel surfing?

24.   How do binocular cues differ from monocular cues? How do these types of cues provide information about depth and distance?

25.   What are two systems that appear involved in processing movement?

26.   How is size constancy involved in the Müller-Lyer illusion and the Ponzo illusion? In what ways do culture and experience affect susceptibility to these illusions?

27.   How can bottom-up and top-down processing be viewed as complementary approaches?

28.   How do context and schemas influence the interpretation of experience?

PART TWO: REVIEW AND LEARN
Key Terms, Fill-In Exercises, Application and Using What You Have Learned

Before doing the exercises below, review the information you learned in this chapter. Reread the work you did in part one of this study guide chapter, plus the interim summaries and end-of-chapter summary in your textbook. Review any problem areas. Once you feel comfortable with the material, do the following exercises without referring to your notes or textbook. If you have difficulty with a term or question, mark it and come back to it. When you have finished an exercise, go back to your notes and the textbook to find the answers to the questions that gave you difficulty. Finally, check your answers (key terms against the textbook and the rest against the answer key).

KEY TERMS

Sensation   _____

_____

Perception   _____

_____

Psychophysics _____

_____

Sensory receptors   _____

_____

Transduction   _____

_____

Absolute threshold   _____

_____

Response bias _____

_____

Difference threshold _____

_____

Weber's law _____

_____

Fechner's law _____

_____

Stevens's power law _____

_____

Sensory adaptation _____

_____

Wavelengths _____

_____

Cornea _____

_____

Pupil _____

_____

Iris _____

_____

Lens _____

_____

Accommodation _____

_____

Retina _____

_____

Rods _____

_____

Cones _____

_____

Bipolar cells _____

_____

Ganglion cells _____

_____

Optic nerve _____

_____

Fovea _____

_____

Blind spot _____

_____

Receptive field _____

_____

Blindsight _____

_____

Feature detectors _____

_____

"What" pathway _____

_____

"Where" pathway _____

_____

Hue _____

_____

Young-Helmholtz (trichromatic) theory of color _____

_____

Opponent-process theory _____

_____

Audition_____

_____

Sound waves _____

_____

Cycle _____

_____

Hertz (Hz) _____

_____

Frequency _____

_____

Pitch _____

_____

Complexity _____

_____

Timbre _____

_____

Amplitude _____

_____

Decibels (Db) _____

_____

Eardrum (tympanic membrane) _____

_____

Cochlea _____

_____

Hair cells _____

_____

Auditory nerve _____

_____

Place theory _____

_____

Frequency theory _____

_____

Sound localization _____

_____

Olfaction   _____

_____

Pheromones   _____

_____

Olfactory epithelium   _____

_____

Olfactory nerve _____

_____

Gustation   _____

_____

Taste buds   _____

_____

Phantom limbs _____

_____

Gate-control theory   _____

_____

Proprioceptive senses_____

_____

Vestibular sense   _____

_____

Kinesthesia   _____

_____

Perceptual organization _____

_____

Form perception _____

_____

Figure-ground perception _____

_____

Similarity _____

_____

Proximity _____

_____

Good continuation _____

_____

Simplicity _____

_____

Closure _____

_____

Recognition-by-components _____

_____

Perceptual illusions _____

_____

Depth (or distance) perception _____

_____

Binocular cues _____

_____

Monocular cues   _____

_____

Binocular cells _____

_____

Motion parallax _____

_____

Motion perception   _____

_____

Motion detectors   _____

_____

Perceptual constancy   _____

_____

Color constancy_____

_____

Shape constancy   _____

_____

Size constancy _____

_____

Müller–Lyer illusion   _____

_____

Perceptual interpretation _____

_____

Direct perception   _____

_____

Visual cliff   _____

_____

Bottom-up processing   _____

_____

Top-down processing   _____

_____

Schemas   _____

_____

FILL-IN EXERCISES

Fill in the word or words that best fit in the spaces below.

1.   _____ are immediate experiences of qualities -- such as red, hot, bright, and so forth – whereas _____ are experiences of objects or events that appear to have form, order, or meaning.

2.   The _____ world – the world as subjectively experienced by an individual -- is a joint product of external reality and the person's creative efforts to understand and depict it mentally.

3.   The minimal amount of physical energy needed for an observer to notice a stimulus is called a(n) _____ _____.

4.   The _____ _____ is the lowest level of stimulation required to sense that a change in stimulation has occurred.

5.   _____ law states that as the perceived intensity of a stimulus grows arithmetically, the actual magnitude of the stimulus grows exponentially.

6.   The retina contains two types of photoreceptors: _____ which respond to color, as well as black and white, and _____ which produce visual sensations in black, white, and gray, only.

7.   Hubel and Wiesel discovered _____ _____ in the cortex, specialized neurons that fire only when stimulation in their receptive field matches a very specific pattern.

8.   The three psychological dimensions of color are _____, _____, and _____.

9.   Young adults can hear frequencies from about _____ to about _____ Hertz (Hz), but, as with most senses, capacity diminishes with age.

10.   The process of hearing begins in the _____ ear, where sound waves are funneled into the ear by the _____, the skin-covered cartilage that protrudes from the sides of the head.

11.   Failure of the outer or middle ear to conduct sound to the receptors in the hair cells is called _____ loss. Failure of receptors in the inner ear or of neurons in any auditory pathway in the brain is referred to as _____ loss.

12.   Transduction of taste occurs in the _____ _____, most of which are located on the bumps on the surface of the tongue, called _____.

13.   The gustatory system responds to four basic tastes: _____, _____, _____, and _____.

14.   Sensitivity to pressure varies considerably over the surface of the body. The most sensitive regions are the _____ and _____, and the least sensitive are the _____ and _____.

15.   Of all of the senses, _____ is probably the most affected by beliefs, expectations, and emotional states, and the least reducible to level of stimulation.

16.   Aside from the five traditional senses -- vision, hearing, smell, taste, and touch -- two additional proprioceptive senses, namely _____ and the _____ sense, provide information about the body's position and movement.

17.   _____ _____ refers to the organization of sensations into meaningful shapes and patterns.

18.   The monocular cue of _____ occurs when one object blocks part of another, leading to perception of the obstructed object as more distant.

19.   The visual perception of movement begins in the retina itself, with ganglion cells called _____ _____ that are particularly sensitive to movement.

20.   Generating meaning from sensory experience is the task of _____ _____.

21.   Experience with the environment shapes perceptual interpretation by creating perceptual expectations, called _____ _____.

USING WHAT YOU HAVE LEARNED

Having just studied the topics of sensation and perception, you likely have a great deal of new insight into a number of "real life" questions that puzzle a lot of people. Based on what you have read, address each of the following questions.

1.   When the lights come on in the theater at the end of a movie, why do they seem so much brighter than when you first entered the theater before the movie started?

2.   Does an X-ray of your leg actually look different to a radiologist than to the average person?

3.   When you first walk into a crowded room, why does the noise seem unbearable, but after a few minutes, you hardly even notice it?

4.   Why can your dog hear a "silent" dog whistle, while you can't?

5.   Is grass really green, to a cow?

6.   How are blind people able to read the raised dots that constitute Braille?

7.   Why is it that whenever you have a head-cold and cannot smell because of your stuffy nose, all the food you eat tastes bland?

8.   Why does a needle seem to hurt less when the doctor distracts you by talking or telling a joke?

9.   How is it that you can see colored images on your color television?

10.   Why does your singing sound so much better in the shower than it sounds out of the shower?

APPLICATION

Situation

You've been lucky to land a job assisting a cross-cultural psychologist interested in how spatial perception in people from a non-Western culture differs from that of individuals from Western society. She has been conducting research recently with a group of people living in an isolated mountain community with no roads, no television, and little contact with outsiders. Several of them agree to participate in your research. It's exciting to have the opportunity to examine spatial perception from a cross-cultural perspective.

Questions to Answer

1.   How would you expect the three-dimensional perceptual abilities of these participants to compare with those of individuals from your own culture?

2.   These individuals have had no exposure to Western architecture. What influence might this have on their perceptual abilities? Compared with an individual from a city, would you expect them to be more or less susceptible to the *Müller-Lyer* illusion? What about the *Ponzo* illusion? Why?

3.   If, as young children, these individuals had participated in research employing the "visual cliff" apparatus, how would you have expected them to react? According to Gibson's theory of direct perception, how would they react compared to children reared in Western society?

4.   Based on your research, what conclusions would you likely draw regarding the influence of culture and experience on perception?

PART THREE: TEST AND KNOW
SAMPLE TEST QUESTIONS

Test how well you have learned this chapter's material by answering the sample test questions. You may wish to mark your answers on a separate sheet of paper so you can reuse this test for exam review. Once you have completed the exam, check your answers and then go back to your notes and the textbook to review questions you found difficult.

1.   Which of the following features is **not** shared by all sensory modalities?

   a.   a one-to-one correspondence between physical and psychological reality
   b.   the ability to translate physical stimulation into sensory signals
   c.   the ability to detect changes in stimulation
   d.   a specific threshold -- below which a person does not sense anything, despite external stimulation

2.   Johannes Müller proposed that whether a neural message is experienced as light, sound, or some other sensation results less from differences in stimuli than from the particular neurons excited by them. This hypothesis is known as:

a.   the Müller–Lyer illusion   b.   Müller's law
c.   opponent-process theory   d.   the doctrine of specific nerve energies

3.   One type of correct response that may be given by subjects participating in a signal detection experiment is a correct negative. In this event, the subject would report

a.   a stimulus when an actual stimulus was presented
b.   a stimulus when no actual stimulus was presented
c.   no stimulus when no actual stimulus was presented
d.   no stimulus, when an actual stimulus was presented

4.   Focusing in the eye occurs in the

a.   iris   b.   retina
c.   lens   d.   aqueous humor

5.   The central region of the retina, which is most sensitive to small detail and provides sharpest vision for stimuli directly in sight, is the

a.   vitreous humor   b.   fovea
c.   rods   d.   optic nerve

6.   Transduction in the eye starts with

a.   impulses from the optic nerve passing through the optic tracts
b.   visual information traveling to the primary visual cortex, in the occipital lobes
c.   neurons in the lateral geniculate nucleus receiving input from the reticular formation
d.   the focusing of images onto the retina

7.   A neurologist has just shown Samir an object, but Samir denies seeing it. Yet, when asked to describe the geometrical form of the object, Samir is able to do so with accuracy far better than one would expect simply by chance. The neurologist is likely to diagnose Samir as suffering from

a.   amnesia.   b.   blindsight.
c.   blindness.   d.   kinesthesia.

8.   Which of the following theories argues that all colors are derived from three color systems: a black-white system, a blue-yellow system, and a red-green system?

a.   place theory   b.   opponent-process theory
c.   Stevens's power law   d.   the doctrine of specific nerve energies

9. When blue and yellow paints are mixed, green is produced. This is because:

   a. only the wavelengths not absorbed by *either* the blue or the yellow pigments reach the eye, which is what we perceive as green.
   b. the wavelengths produced by blue and yellow pigments combine in the retina to give the impression of green.
   c. the increase in saturation resulting from the combination of these two primary colors gives the impression of green.
   d. blue, yellow, and red are primary colors according to the *trichromatic theory of color*. All other colors result from the mixing of these primary colors.

10. People recognize each other's voices, as well as the sounds of different musical instruments, from their characteristic

a.	frequency	b.	pitch
c.	timbre	d.	amplitude

11. The outer boundary of the middle ear is marked by the _____.

a.	eustachian tube	b.	cochlea
c.	malleus	d.	tympanic membrane

12. In terms of sensing pitch, *place theory* holds that

    a. different areas of the basilar membrane are maximally sensitive to different frequencies
    b. the more frequently a sound wave cycles, the more frequently the basilar membrane vibrates and hair cells fire
    c. neurons may stagger their responses, so that the combined pattern produces a signal of a particular frequency
    d. the location or place from which a sound originates can be identified by means of sound localization

13. Gustatory information travels to one of two destinations in the brain: one via the thalamus to the primary gustatory cortex, and the other to the limbic system. People with damage to the cortical first pathway, but not to the second

    a. fail to identify substances by taste, but react with appropriate affective and behavioral responses to tastes
    b. can identify substances by taste, but fail to show appropriate affective or behavioral response to tastes
    c. cannot identify substances by taste and fail to react with the appropriate affective and behavioral responses to tastes
    d. can identify substances by taste and show an immediate affective or behavioral response to tastes

14.   The approximately _____ square feet of skin covering the human body constitutes a complex, multilayered organ.

a.   2   b.   10
c.   18   d.   25

15.   People spend billions of dollars a year fighting pain, but pain serves an important function in that

a.   it builds character
b.   it prevents tissue damage
c.   it indicates the presence of the disorder "painful neuropathy"
d.   it distracts us from the worries of modern life

16.   Chronic pain patients tend to

a.   blame their physical condition for all life's difficulties, while denying emotional and interpersonal problems
b.   be anxious, needy, and dependent
c.   have difficulty expressing anger
d.   all of the above

17.   The two organs that transduce vestibular information are called _____, and are located _____.

a.   the semicircular canals and the vestibular sacs; in the inner ear
b.   the tendons and the muscles; in the joints
c.   the pinna and the tympanic membrane; in the outer ear
d.   kinesthesia and the vestibular sense; the medulla

18.   Which of the following is *not* a major perceptual rule by which the brain automatically and unconsciously organizes sensory input into meaningful wholes, as proposed by Gestalt psychologists?

a.   proximity   b.   shading
c.   good continuation   d.   simplicity

19.   Generating meaning from sensory experience is the task of

a.   perceptual organization   b.   direct perception
c.   perceptual interpretation   d.   perceptual constancy

20.   According to current thinking, perception involves

a.   top-down processing   b.   bottom-up processing
c.   both of the above   d.   neither of the above

ANSWERS

FILL-IN EXERCISES

1. sensations; perceptions 2. phenomenological 3. absolute threshold 4. difference threshold
5. Stevens's power 6. cones; rods 7. feature detectors 8. hue, saturation, lightness 9. 15; 20,000
10. outer; pinna 11. conduction; sensorineural 12. taste buds; papillae 13. sweet, sour, salty, bitter
14. face, fingers; back, legs 15. pain 16. kinesthesia; vestibular 17. form perception 18. interposition
19. motion detectors 20. perceptual interpretation 21. perceptual set

APPLICATION

1. Their experience with binocular and many monocular cues would provide information about depth. Their depth perception should, therefore, be as good as that of anyone else.

2. Lack of roads joining at angles, rectangular buildings, and so on would result in less experience with the kinds of cues that give rise to Müller-Lyer illusion. Lack of experience with lines converging in the distance (e.g., roads, railway tracks) would lead to less susceptibility to Ponzo illusion.

3. As they began to crawl, they would have been reluctant to cross to the deep side of the cliff. According to Gibson's theory, both the understanding of depth cues and the meaning of falling off the cliff may be inborn in humans.

4. Early experience shapes the neural systems underlying sensation and perception. Some perceptual abilities are influenced by culture-specific experiences (e.g., architecture and angles); others seem uninfluenced by culture (e.g., avoidance of deep side on visual cliff) and may even be innate.

SAMPLE TEST QUESTIONS

1.	a	11.	d
2.	d	12.	a
3.	c	13.	a
4.	c	14.	c
5.	b	15.	b
6.	d	16.	d
7.	b	17.	a
8.	b	18.	b
9.	a	19.	c
10.	c	20.	c

Chapter 5
Learning

PART ONE: PRE-READ AND WORK
Outline and Learning Objectives

Pre-read this chapter's table of contents and end-of-chapter summary. Then, use the outline segment-by-segment to help you work through the chapter. Jot down your own questions, comments, and notes in the space provided. Make a note of key terms and of difficult areas that you will need to review (include page numbers). Then, answer the questions in the learning objectives section that follows. Check off those you are confident that you can answer well. Re-read the material in the text for the questions about which you are less confident. Record the important points from your reading in the space below each question.

OUTLINE

Classical Conditioning

Pavlov's Model

Conditioned Responses

Stimulus Generalization and Discrimination

Extinction

Factors That Affect Classical Conditioning

What Do Organisms Learn in Classical Conditioning?

From Brain to Behavior: The Neural Basis of Classical Conditioning

Operant Conditioning

Reinforcement

Punishment

Extinction

Operant Conditioning of Complex Behaviors

One Step Further: Why Are Reinforcers Reinforcing?

Cognitive-Social Theory

Learning and Cognition

A Global Vista: Optimism, Pessimism, and Expectancies of Control in Cross-Cultural Perspective

Social Learning

Central Questions: What Have We Learned About Learning?

LEARNING OBJECTIVES

Upon completion of Chapter 5, you should be able to answer the following questions.

1. What are the three assumptions shared by theories of learning?

2. What are the basic principles underlying Pavlov's model of conditioning?

3. What are the differences between an unconditioned stimulus (UCS) and a conditioned stimulus (CS), and between an unconditioned response (UCR) and a conditioned response (CR)?

4. How did John Watson produce a conditioned emotional response in little Albert?

5. How can the functioning of the immune system be affected by classical conditioning?

6. How does stimulus generalization differ from stimulus discrimination?

7. What is involved in the processes of extinction and spontaneous recovery?

8.   Discuss the notion that animals may be biologically prepared to learn some associations more easily than others.

9.   What is the phenomenon of paradoxical conditioning?

10.   Explain how research suggests that learning occurs through changes in the strength of connections between neurons.

11.   How does reinforcement differ from punishment? Provide illustrations of positive and negative reinforcement, as well as positive and negative punishment.

12.   How does operant learning theory explain superstitious behavior?

13.   What are five common drawbacks associated with the use of punishment?

14.   How does partial reinforcement differ from continuous reinforcement? Describe four types of partial reinforcement schedules and their effects on responding.

15.   Provide several everyday examples of discriminative stimuli signaling the occurrence of particular contingencies of reinforcement.

16.   Explain what is meant by the term "behavioral economics."

17.   How can shaping and chaining be used to teach complex behaviors?

18.   How does drive reduction account for the reinforcing value of certain stimuli?

19.   How do secondary reinforcers acquire their reinforcing properties?

20.   What are the roles of the behavioral approach system (BAS) and the behavioral inhibition system (BIS) in the learning of operant behavior?

21.   How does the phenomenon of latent learning provide evidence for the role of cognition in learning?

22.   What is meant by the term locus of control? How do people with an internal locus of control differ from those with an external locus of control?

23.   In what ways do individuals with a pessimistic explanatory style interpret negative events in a depressive manner?

24.   What is involved in the phenomenon of social learning and how is this important in the cognitive social theory of learning?

25.   How can a person learn the consequences of behavior through the process of vicarious conditioning?

PART TWO: REVIEW AND LEARN
Key Terms, Fill-In Exercises, Application and Using What You Have Learned

Before doing the exercises below, review the information you learned in this chapter. Reread the work you did in part one of this study guide chapter, plus the interim summaries and end-of-chapter summary in your textbook. Review any problem areas. Once you feel comfortable with the material, do the following exercises without referring to your notes or textbook. If you have difficulty with a term or question, mark it and come back to it. When you have finished an exercise, go back to your notes and the textbook to find the answers to the questions that gave you difficulty. Finally, check your answers (key terms against the textbook and the rest against the answer key).

KEY TERMS

Learning _____

_____

Reflex _____

_____

Stimulus _____

_____

Habituation _____

_____

Laws of association _____

_____

Classical conditioning _____

_____

Conditioning _____

_____

Unconditioned stimulus (UCS) _____

_____

Unconditioned response (UCR) _____

_____

Conditioned response (CR) _____

_____

Conditioned stimulus (CS) _____

_____

Phobias _____

_____

Immune system _____

_____

Stimulus generalization _____

_____

Galvanic skin response (GSR) _____

_____

Stimulus discrimination _____

_____

Extinction _____

_____

Spontaneous recovery _____

_____

Interstimulus interval _____

_____

Blocking _____

_____

Latent inhibition _____

_____

Prepared learning _____

_____

Long-term potentiation _____

_____

Law of effect _____

_____

Operant conditioning _____

_____

Operants _____

_____

Reinforcement _____

_____

Punishment _____

_____

Reinforcer _____

_____

Positive reinforcement _____

_____

Positive reinforcer _____

_____

Superstitious behavior _____

_____

Negative reinforcement _____

_____

Negative reinforcer _____

_____

Escape learning_____

_____

Avoidance learning _____

_____

Continuous reinforcement schedule _____

_____

Partial or intermittent schedule of reinforcement _____

_____

Ratio schedules_____

_____

Interval schedules _____

_____

Fixed ratio (FR) schedule   _____

_____

Variable ratio (VR) schedule   _____

_____

Fixed interval (FI) schedule   _____

_____

Variable interval (VI) schedule   _____

_____

Discriminative stimulus (S^D)   _____

_____

Shaping   _____

_____

Biofeedback   _____

_____

Chaining   _____

_____

Drive   _____

_____

Drive-reduction theory   _____

_____

Primary reinforcers   _____

_____

Secondary reinforcers _____

_____

Behavioral approach system (BAS) _____

_____

Behavioral inhibition system (BIS) _____

_____

Fight-flight system _____

_____

Cognitive-social theory _____

_____

Cognitive maps _____

_____

Latent learning _____

_____

Insight _____

_____

Expectancies _____

_____

Generalized expectancies _____

_____

Locus of control of reinforcement _____

_____

Internal locus of control _____

_____

External locus of control _____

_____

Learned helplessness _____

_____

Explanatory style   _____

_____

Pessimistic explanatory style _____

_____

Social learning _____

_____

Observational learning _____

_____

Modeling   _____

_____

Vicarious conditioning _____

_____

Tutelage   _____

_____

FILL-IN EXERCISES

Fill in the word or words that best fit in the spaces below.

1. Classical conditioning involves associating a neutral stimulus with the _____ stimulus. Following several trials, the neutral stimulus will come to elicit the response, and is now referred to as the _____ stimulus.

2. The fear response that little Albert displayed to the white rat in Watson and Rayner's study is an example of a _____ _____ response.

3. Little Albert's fear of other stimuli that shared certain characteristics with the rat (i.e., furry or hairy objects) is a good example of the phenomenon of _____ _____.

4. Galvanic skin response (GSR) is an electrical measure of the amount of sweat on the skin and can be used to assess _____.

5. Each pairing of the CS and UCS is know as a conditioning _____.

6. Presentation of the CS without the UCS will lead to _____ of the CR.

7. The duration of time between presentation of the CS and UCS is referred to as the _____ _____.

8. The failure of a stimulus to elicit a conditioned response when it is combined with another stimulus that is already effective in eliciting the response is called _____.

9. Fear of snakes and spiders in humans may involve the learning of associations that are biologically _____.

10. _____ _____ refers to the tendency of a group of neurons to fire more readily after consistent stimulation from other neurons.

11. Operants are behaviors that are _____ by the organism rather than _____ by the environment.

12. Negative reinforcement _____ the probability that a response will occur.

13. The unannounced, unexpected arrival of the health inspector at the door of the neighborhood restaurant is an example of a _____ _____ schedule of reinforcement.

14. Psychologists use _____ to help patients to gain control over autonomic responses such as heart rate, body temperature, and blood pressure by feeding them information about these responses.

15.   A _____ is a state that impels the organism to act.

16.   _____ _____ refers to the expectancy that one cannot escape aversive events, which leads to motivational and learning deficits.

USING WHAT YOU HAVE LEARNED

One of the most difficult problems parents face is when their children display temper tantrums. Kids will scream, roll around on the floor, bang their hands and heads on the floor, hold their breath, and so on until they get what they want. Parents are often embarrassed or concerned that their child might hurt himself or herself. So they often "give in" and let the child have what he or she wanted in order to end the tantrum.

In terms of reinforcement, what do you suppose happens when parents give in to the tantrum? How will this likely affect the probability of future tantrums?

If giving in stops the tantrum (an aversive stimulus), what are parents likely to do the next time the child throws a tantrum? Why?

Often, children learn that there are certain places where parents will give in quickly, such as on the bus or in a quiet place like a library. Kids are all the more likely to throw a tantrum in these places. What do these situations signal to the child? What would be the behavioral term to apply to these situations?

What would you advise parents to do to stop the tantrums, based on your understanding of the principles of learning?

APPLICATION

Situation

After his class attended a special kids' performance of the symphony, 8-year-old Billy had been begging his parents to buy him a violin. Finally, they gave in and got him one. The only problem is that he doesn't practice. His teacher says he should practice for half an hour each day, but Billy never does more than 5 minutes. His mom keeps nagging him to practice, but it doesn't work. He practices for 5 minutes, and then he's off to his friend's house. His mom is getting frustrated and is considering canceling his lessons. Having just studied learning in her psychology course, she decides to try applying operant learning principles to change Billy's behavior. She buys a Nintendo, to use to reward Billy for practicing for half an hour each day. She realizes, however, that half an hour of practice will initially seem like an eternity to him, and he'll probably give up after only 10 minutes. So, she gets her kitchen timer and tells Billy: "I want you to practice your violin until the bell on the timer rings. When it rings, come and get me and we'll play Nintendo together." The first day, she sets the timer for 5 minutes. The next day, she sets it for 10 minutes. The next day she sets it for 15 minutes, and so on. By the end of the week, Billy is practicing for half an hour.

Questions to Answer

1.   In the above situation, playing Nintendo with mom serves as what?

2.   Rewarding Billy for practicing his violin for a progressively longer time is an example of what?

3.   The bell on the timer serves as what kind of stimulus?

After a couple of weeks, Billy's mom is pleased that he is practicing for half an hour a day, but is finding that she hasn't got the time to play Nintendo with him every day. Yet, when she told him she hasn't got time to play Nintendo any more, Billy's practicing time dropped back to 5 minutes.

4.   Billy's drop in practice time after his mom stopped playing Nintendo with him is an example of what principle of learning?

5.   In terms of operant learning theory, how could Billy's mom cut back on playing Nintendo, but still keep Billy regularly practicing for half an hour?

PART THREE:　TEST AND KNOW
SAMPLE TEST QUESTIONS

Test how well you have learned this chapter's material by answering the sample test questions. You may wish to mark your answers on a separate sheet of paper so you can reuse this test for exam review. Once you have completed the exam, check your answers and then go back to your notes and the textbook to review questions you found difficult.

1. Praise is a good example of a(n)

   a. conditioned stimulus
   b. unconditioned stimulus
   c. secondary reinforcer
   d. vicarious reinforcer

2. Slot machines are popular in casinos because all you have to do to play is pull the lever. Every so often, after an unpredictable number of pulls, somebody will "hit the jackpot." What schedule of reinforcement is likely in effect here?

   a. fixed interval
   b. fixed ratio
   c. variable interval
   d. variable ratio

3. The fact that people will put money into slot machines and pull the level over and over, especially after seeing someone else hit the jackpot, even though they may have never won anything themselves can be explained in terms of

   a. vicarious learning
   b. avoidance learning
   c. classical conditioning
   d. operant conditioning

4. Tolman suggested that rats may form _____ , or mental representations of a maze, even without any reinforcement.

   a. cognitive maps
   b. generalized expectancies
   c. outcome expectancies
   d. all of the above

5. Many people display severe negative emotional reactions to hypodermic needles, through exposure to injections in childhood. These reactions can be explained in terms of:

   a. instrumental conditioning
   b. classical conditioning
   c. blocking
   d. preparedness to learn

6.   Suppose Watson and Raynor had exposed little Albert repeatedly (i.e., on the second, third, and all subsequent trials) to the white rat but without the noise.

   a.   Albert's fear response would have become even stronger.
   b.   Albert's fear response would have generalized to whatever white, furry objects were present in the environment.
   c.   Albert's fear response would have extinguished.
   d.   Albert's fear response would have spontaneously recovered.

7.   In classical conditioning, the most effective form of temporal relationship between the CS and UCS involves

   a.   forward conditioning   b.   backward conditioning
   c.   simultaneous conditioning   d.   paradoxical conditioning

8.   The sight of drug paraphernalia can activate physiological reactions that reduce the effect of the heroin an addict is about to take. This likely involves

   a.   stimulus substitution   b.   escape learning
   c.   vicarious conditioning   d.   paradoxical conditioning

9.   Learning to drive a car with a manual transmission involves acquiring a variety of behaviors, such as shifting the gears, using the clutch, using the accelerator, and so on. Putting these together to drive the car smoothly involves

   a.   chaining
   b.   escape learning
   c.   shaping
   d.   simultaneous conditioning

10.   Keeping your driving speed below the speed limit so you don't get caught in a radar trap is an example of

   a.   avoidance learning
   b.   escape learning
   c.   shaping
   d.   positive punishment

11.   Removing a child's TV privileges is an example of

   a.   negative reinforcement
   b.   negative punishment
   c.   positive punishment
   d.   secondary reinforcement

12. Punishment tends to be most effective

   a.   when it is severe
   b.   when it occurs some time after the behavior
   c.   when it is accompanied by reasoning
   d.   punishment is *never* effective

13. The students in Mr. Bebby's grade 8 class have learned not to fool around when he's mad, because he's likely to give the whole class detention. The easiest way to tell when he's mad is that you can see a vein on the side of his forehead begin throbbing. When that vein starts throbbing, the students immediately settle down. Mr. Bebby's throbbing vein is a

   a.   secondary reinforcer
   b.   conditioned stimulus
   c.   conditioned response
   d.   discriminative stimulus

14. In the above example, settling down when Mr. Bebby's vein starts throbbing is an example of

   a.   superstitious behavior
   b.   a conditioned response
   c.   avoidance learning
   d.   latent learning

15. Gray argues that anatomically distinct pathways in the nervous system control different forms of learning and are associated with different emotional states. The system involved in negative reinforcement and punishment is

   a.   the behavioral approach system
   b.   the behavioral inhibition system
   c.   the fight-flight system
   d.   the latent inhibition system

16. Learning that has occurred, but is not currently manifest in behavior, was described by Tolman as

   a.   latent learning
   b.   discriminative learning
   c.   vicarious learning
   d.   escape learning

17. Everything has been going wrong for Ted. No matter what he tries, it doesn't seem to make any difference. So, he's just given up trying. Ted's behavior is an example of

   a.   avoidance learning   b.   paradoxical conditioning
   c.   stimulus generalization   d.   learned helplessness

18. All of the following *except* one are ways in which individuals with a pessimistic explanatory style see the causes of negative events. Which does not apply?

   a. internal
   b. stable
   c. global
   d. temporary

19. Fishing involves behavior that is difficult to extinguish. People who like fishing will spend hours "on the lake" without catching anything, before finally giving up in frustration. This is because fishing likely involves

   a. a conditioned emotional response
   b. backward conditioning
   c. intermittent reinforcement
   d. tutelage

20. After seeing a child get bitten by a dog, little Mario displays an intense fear reaction when he sees a puppy at the pet store. His response can be explained with reference to

   a. classical conditioning
   b. vicarious conditioning
   c. instrumental conditioning
   d. negative reinforcement

ANSWERS

FILL-IN EXERCISES

1. unconditioned; conditioned   2. conditioned emotional 3. stimulus generalization 4. arousal (or anxiety)
5. trial 6. extinction   7. interstimulus interval   8. blocking 9. prepared   10. long-term potentiation
11. emitted; elicited   12. increases 13. variable interval 14. biofeedback 15. drive 16. learned
helplessness

APPLICATION

1. A positive reinforcer 2. Shaping 3. A discriminative stimulus 4. Extinction
5. Partial reinforcement (variable ratio schedule)

SAMPLE TEST QUESTIONS

1.	c	11.	b
2.	d	12.	c
3.	a	13.	d
4.	a	14.	c
5.	b	15.	b
6.	c	16.	a
7.	a	17.	d
8.	d	18.	d
9.	a	19.	c
10.	a	20.	b

Chapter 6
Memory

PART ONE: PRE-READ AND WORK
Outline and Learning Objectives

Pre-read this chapter's table of contents and end-of-chapter summary. Then, use the outline segment-by-segment to help you work through the chapter. Jot down your own questions, comments, and notes in the space provided. Make a note of difficult areas that you will need to review (include page numbers). Then, answer the questions in the learning objectives section that follows. Check off those you are confident that you can answer well. Re-read the material in the text for the questions about which you are less confident. Record the important points from your reading in the space below each question.

OUTLINE

Memory and Information Processing

Mental Representations

Information Processing: An Evolving Model

Working Memory

Processing Information in Working Memory: The Central Executive

Visual and Verbal Storage

One Step Further: The Neuropsychology of Working Memory

The Relation Between Working Memory and Long-Term Memory

Varieties of Long-Term Memory

Declarative and Procedural Memory

Explicit and Implicit Memory

From Brain to Behavior: The Neuropsychology of Long-Term Memory

Everyday Memory

Encoding and Organization of Long-Term Memory

Encoding

Mnemonic Devices

Networks of Association

Schemas

Remembering, Misremembering, and Forgetting

How Long is Long-Term Memory?

How Accurate is Long-Term Memory?

Why do People Forget?

Commentary: Repressed Memories of Sexual Abuse

Central Questions: What is Memory?

LEARNING OBJECTIVES

Upon completion of Chapter 6, you should be able to answer the following questions.

1. In what ways do sensory representations differ from verbal representations?

2. How does iconic storage differ from echoic storage?

3. What are the major differences between long-term and short-term memory?

4. How does serial position affect free recall?

5. What are four major ways in which thinking about memory has evolved over the past decade?

6. Discuss the storage and processing functions of working memory.

7. What evidence does neurological research provide for the notion of working memory?

8. How are working memory and long-term memory related?

9. What are the differences between declarative and procedural memory?

10. How does explicit memory differ from implicit memory?

11. Does neurological research support the distinction between explicit and implicit memory?

12.   What has recent research revealed about everyday memory?

13.   How is the accessibility of information in long-term memory influenced by the following: level of processing, spacing, and representational modes?

14.   What are two common forms of mnemonic devices?

15.   Explain how pieces of information stored in memory form networks of association.

16.   In what ways is hierarchical organization of information analogous to a filing system?

17.   How are both encoding and retrieval of information affected by schemas?

18.   How can the organization of information in memory be influenced by culture?

19.   Why are some researchers concerned about the accuracy of eyewitness testimony in the courtroom?

20.   What are the differences between the following three explanations of forgetting: decay, interference, and motivated forgetting?

21.   Why is it difficult to scientifically address the issue of false memories of childhood trauma?

PART TWO: REVIEW AND LEARN
Key Terms, Fill-In Exercises, Application and Using What You Have Learned

Before doing the exercises below, review the information you learned in this chapter. Reread the work you did in part one of this study guide chapter, plus the interim summaries and end-of-chapter summary in your textbook. Review any problem areas. Once you feel comfortable with the material, do the following exercises without referring to your notes or textbook. If you have difficulty with a term or question, mark it and come back to it. When you have finished an exercise, go back to your notes and the textbook to find the answers to the questions that gave you difficulty. Finally, check your answers (key terms against the textbook and the rest against the answer key).

KEY TERMS

Upon completion of Chapter 6, you should be able to define the following terms.

Sensory representations _____

_____

Verbal representations _____

_____

Sensory registers   _____

_____

Iconic storage   _____

_____

Echoic storage _____

_____

Short-term memory (STM)   _____

_____

Rehearsal _____

_____

Maintenance rehearsal _____

_____

Elaborative rehearsal _____

_____

Long-term memory _____

_____

Retrieval _____

_____

Serial position effect _____

_____

Memory systems _____

_____

Working memory _____

_____

Chunking _____

_____

Declarative memory _____

_____

Semantic memory _____

_____

Episodic memory   _____

_____

Procedural memory   _____

_____

Explicit memory _____

_____

Implicit memory _____

_____

Recall   _____

_____

Tip-of-the-tongue phenomenon   _____

_____

Recognition   _____

_____

Priming effects   _____

_____

Everyday memory   _____

_____

Retrospective memory   _____

_____

Prospective memory   _____

_____

Encoding _____

_____

Level of processing _____

_____

Encoding specificity principle _____

_____

Retrieval cues _____

_____

Spacing effect _____

_____

Mnemonic devices _____

_____

Method of loci _____

_____

SQ3R method _____

_____

Networks of association _____

_____

Nodes _____

_____

Spreading activation theory _____

_____

Cultural models _____

_____

Forgetting   _____

_____

Flashbulb memories   _____

_____

Decay theory   _____

_____

Interference   _____

_____

Proactive interference   _____

_____

Retroactive interference _____

_____

Motivated forgetting   _____

_____

FILL-IN EXERCISES

Fill in the word or words that best fit in the spaces below.

1.   People maintain a mental image (icon) of what they have seen that lasts for approximately _____ to _____ seconds.

2.   To assess _____ _____, psychologists often measure subjects' digit span; that is, how many numbers they can hold in memory at once.

3.   Short-term memory holds information in consciousness for approximately _____ to _____ seconds, unless the person makes a deliberate attempt to retain it longer by repeating it over and over.

4.   On the average, people can hold about _____ pieces of information in STM, with the normal range from _____ to _____ items.

5.   The tendency for subjects to remember words at the beginning of a list better than words that appear later is known as the _____ effect.

6.   Information remains in _____ memory only so long as the person is consciously processing, examining, or manipulating it.

7.   According to one prominent model, working memory consists of three memory systems: a _____ memory store, a _____ memory store, and a _____ _____ that controls and manipulates the information that these two short-term stores hold in mind.

8.   Memory for facts and events, much of which can be consciously stated, is referred to as _____ memory.

9.   Semantic memory is also referred to as _____ memory by some psychologists.

10.   Memory that is expressed in behavior but does not require conscious recollection is referred to as _____ memory.

11.   Neurological research indicates that the neural structure known as the _____ is central to the consolidation of explicit memories.

12.   _____ memory has at least two components: remembering *to* remember (or *intent*) and remembering *what* to remember (or *content*).

13.   According to the _____ _____ principle, the contexts in which people encode and retrieve information can affect the ease of retrieval.

14.   _____ devices are strategies that people use as memory aids.

15.   Networks of association involve complex interconnections among _____.

16.   The filing cabinet metaphor suggests that information in LTM tends to be filed _____; that is, broad categories are composed of narrower subcategories, which in turn consist of even more specific categories.

17.   _____ are patterns of thought, or organized knowledge structures that render the environment relatively predictable.

18.   _____ _____ are memories of exciting or highly consequential events.

19.   _____ interference refers to the interference of previous stored memories with the retrieval of new information.

USING WHAT YOU HAVE LEARNED

A group of university students listened to a news report describing how an airline pilot courageously landed a plane safely after its landing gear had failed.

After hearing this story, most of the students described the aircraft as a jet, although there was no mention in the story of what type of aircraft it was. In addition, several of them added details that were not in the news report, such as describing the pilot as male, or adding the observation that it had been raining at the time of the landing.

What type of memory do these phenomena involve? What is likely responsible for the addition of new information about the type of aircraft, the sex of the pilot, and the weather conditions? Have you ever noticed similar errors in your own recall of specific details of events? Could there be any advantage to such aspects of memory?

APPLICATION

Situation

A friend of yours, knowing that you are studying psychology and that you have just finished learning about memory, asks for your advice in how to prepare for an upcoming exam. In terms of what you have covered in this chapter, how would you answer her questions?

1. "When I get into the exam I always just go blank. Are there any 'memory tricks' that will help me remember the important concepts I have to remember?"

2. "I find it best to stay up all night and cram the night before. The only problem is that some of this material will also be on the final next month. Is there a better way to study so that I'll remember more for the final?"

3. "Is it best just to read my notes over and over, or is there some other thing I could be doing?"

4. "Someone told me that it's better to study the material in a different order every time I go over it. You know, tomorrow begin with the material I studied in the middle tonight and end with the beginning material. Next night, begin with the end material. Is there any truth to that? Why would that help?"

5. "Sometimes I find that studying for Italian actually makes it harder to remember the material I previously studied for my French exam. Am I just fooling myself, or could this really happen?"

PART THREE: TEST AND KNOW
SAMPLE TEST QUESTIONS

Test how well you have learned this chapter's material by answering the sample test questions. You may wish to mark your answers on a separate sheet of paper so you can reuse this test for exam review. Once you have completed the exam, check your answers and then go back to your notes and the textbook to review questions you found difficult.

1. Repeating information over and over again to prevent it from fading is a procedure known as

    a.   rehearsal
    b.   chunking
    c.   echoic storage
    d.   SQ3R method

2.   When a list of words is presented to subjects, they tend to remember those at the beginning and at the end of the list more easily than those in the middle, because of

a.   the primacy effect
b.   the serial position effect
c.   the priming process
d.   rehearsal

3.   Baddeley and Hitch had subjects perform two tasks simultaneously: one involved recalling a series of digits and the other involved some kind of thinking, such as reasoning or comprehending the meaning of sentences. Their results suggested that

a.   storage capacity and processing capacity are two separate aspects of working memory
b.   storage capacity and processing capacity are ultimately the same thing; they are highly interdependent
c.   short-term memory is too limited to involve working on two tasks simultaneously
d.   while storage capacity in STM is unlimited, processing capacity is limited to a small number of tasks

4.   Working memory appears to be "orchestrated" by the _____, a region of the brain long known to be involved in most high-level cognitive functions.

a.   hippocampus
b.   hypothalamus
c.   prefrontal cortex
d.   occipital cortex

5.   In a memory experiment involving recall of a series of digits, one subject reported treating the digits like phone numbers, breaking the series down into a 3-digit "area code," a 7-digit "phone number," and a 4-digit "extension." Using this procedure, the subject was able to hold 14 digits in working memory. This procedure is an example of

a.   the method of loci
b.   semantic processing
c.   spacing of rehearsal
d.   chunking

6.   Declarative memory can involve either _____ or _____ memory.

a.   semantic; phonemic
b.   semantic; structural
c.   explicit; implicit
d.   semantic; episodic

7. Multiple choice tests, such as this, likely involve which type of retrieval from LTM?

   a. recognition   b. recall
   c. implicit   d. secondary

8. In a classical conditioning procedure in which a tone is paired with electric shock, patients with an intact hippocampus but a damaged amygdala

   a. have no conscious idea that the tone is associated with shock, but show a conditioned fear response to it nonetheless
   b. consciously know that the tone is associated with shock, and show a conditioned fear response to it
   c. consciously know that the tone is associated with shock, but show no conditioned fear response to it
   d. have no conscious idea that the tone is associated with shock, nor show a conditioned fear response to it

9. Melanie ties a string around her finger in the morning, so she won't forget to pick up a loaf of bread on her way home from work. What aspect of memory is involved in this situation?

   a. working memory
   b. procedural memory
   c. implicit memory
   d. prospective memory

10. Many students report that it is much easier for them to recall information when they write an in-class test in the same room as they take a the course than when they write the final examination in an examination hall or the gym. A possible reason for this difference is

   a. interference
   b. retrieval cues
   c. motivated forgetting
   d. memory decay

11. Driving to school, Maria was mentally rehearsing for her psychology exam. To help remember the important topics for the exam, she created a ridiculous mental image of the topics being scattered around her bedroom -- on the bed, under the pillow, under the bed, on her desk, and so on. As she drove along, she suddenly realized that she had driven 3 miles without even paying attention to her driving. Yet she had not run any red lights, and she had used her clutch properly and not stalled while shifting gears. This unconscious, automatic behavior could be described as involving

   a. declarative memory
   b. implicit memory
   c. episodic memory
   d. short-term memory

12.   Maria's method of trying to remember the important topics for her exam, in the previous question, involves using

    a.   the method of loci
    b.   the SQ3R method
    c.   the deep processing method
    d.   none of the above

13.   The "spacing effect" refers to

    a.   the superiority of memory for information at both the beginning and end of a series
    b.   the superiority of memory for information rehearsed over long intervals
    c.   the superiority of memory for information broken down into chunks
    d.   the *lunch counter* model of STM – there is "limited space" at the counter

14.   Pieces of information along a network of associations are called _____.

    a.   nodes   b.   loci
    c.   files   d.   schemas

15.   Schemas play an important role in helping to process new information and enter it into memory. Schemas can also result in processing and retrieval errors. Which of the following errors could be attributable to schemas?

    a.   leading people to misclassify information
    b.   causing people to believe they have seen information that really was not present
    c.   causing people to fail to notice information that might be important
    d.   all of the above

16.   Research on forgetting shows that

    a.   forgetting follows a typical pattern with a gradual initial loss of information, with the rate of loss increasing with time
    b.   the pace at which information is forgotten is quite different when the time period is hours than when the time period is years
    c.   forgetting follows a typical pattern with a rapid initial loss of information, and only a gradual loss thereafter
    d.   all of the above

17.   Manal remembers sitting with her brother in the living room of her parents' home, wearing her pajamas, when she saw the space shuttle Challenger disaster on TV. Such vivid memories of exciting or highly consequential events are referred to as

    a.   flashbulb memories   b.   iconic memories
    c.   retrospective memories   d.   implicit memories

18.   Dave's voice-mail at the office uses different number keys to play, save, or delete messages than his voice-mail at home. Dave found it very hard to use his office voice-mail. "It just doesn't make sense," he said. "I didn't have this much trouble learning my voice-mail at home. But now I can't get the numbers straight at all!" This problem where previously stored memories interfere with the retrieval of new information is called

    a.   retroactive interference   b.   motivated forgetting
    c.   proactive interference   d.   state-dependent learning

19.   Dave finally learned the new voice-mail at the office. But now, he sometimes can't remember the numbers for his voice-mail at home. This problem is due to

    a.   retroactive interference   b.   repression
    c.   proactive interference   d.   state-dependent learning

20.   _____ refers to the process of explicitly instructing yourself to forget ("Oops, forget that. That's the wrong address. The right address is …").

    a.   proactive interference
    b.   memory decay
    c.   repression
    d.   motivated forgetting

ANSWERS

FILL-IN EXERCISES

1. ½ , two   2. short-term memory   3. 20, 30   4. seven; five, nine   5. primacy   6. working
7. visual; verbal; central executive   8. declarative   9. generic   10. implicit   11. hippocampus
12. prospective   13. encoding specificity   14. mnemonic   15. nodes   16. hierarchically   17. schemas
18. flashbulb memories   19. proactive

APPLICATION

1.   Yes. Use mnemonic devices such as *loci* method and *peg* method.

2.   Yes. Space rehearsal over a period of time.

3.   Don't just read notes over and over. Use encoding strategies. Form associative links to previously
       stored information. Elaborate and reflect upon the information (depth of processing). Use a variety
       of representational modes and mnemonic devices (especially try SQ3R method).

4.   Yes. Serial position effects

5.   Yes. The problem is retroactive interference.

SAMPLE TEST QUESTIONS

1.	a	11.	b
2.	b	12.	a
3.	a	13.	b
4.	c	14.	a
5.	d	15.	d
6.	d	16.	c
7.	a	17.	a
8.	c	18.	c
9.	d	19.	a
10.	b	20.	d

Chapter 7
Thought and Language

PART ONE: PRE-READ AND WORK
Outline and Learning Objectives

Pre-read this chapter's table of contents and end-of-chapter summary. Then, use the outline segment-by-segment to help you work through the chapter. Jot down your own questions, comments, and notes in the space provided. Make a note of difficult areas that you will need to review (include page numbers). Then, answer the questions in the learning objectives section that follows. Check off those you are confident that you can answer well. Re-read the material in the text for the questions about which you are less confident. Record the important points from your reading in the space below each question.

OUTLINE

Units of Thought

Manipulating Mental Representations

Concepts and Categories

A Global Vista: Culture and Categorization

Reasoning, Problem Solving, and Decision Making

Reasoning

Problem Solving

Decision Making

Implicit and Everyday Thinking

How Rational are We?

Implicit Cognition

Emotion, Motivation, and Decision Making

Connectionism

From Brain to Behavior: The Neuropsychology of Thinking

Language

Language and Thought

Transforming Sounds and Symbols into Meaning

The Use of Language in Everyday Life

Language Development

Nature and Nurture in the Development of Language

A Critical Period for Language Development

What Infants Know about Language

From Babbling to Bantering

One Step Further: Is Language Distinctly Human?

Central Questions: What Is So Rational About Reason

LEARNING OBJECTIVES

Upon completion of Chapter 7, you should be able to answer the following questions.

1.   How does thinking employ mental images and mental models?

2.   What are the differences between the prototype-matching and defining-features views of categorization?

3.   How do basic level, subordinate, and superordinate level categories differ?

4.   How is categorization influenced by culture?

5.   How does inductive reasoning differ from deductive reasoning?

6.   How can analogical reasoning be used to help understand a novel situation?

7.   What is the difference between a well-defined and an ill-defined problem?

8.   What are the four steps involved in problem solving?

9.   Describe how algorithms and mental simulation can be used as problem-solving strategies.

10.   In what ways do functional fixedness and the confirmation bias interfere with rational problem solving?

11.   How can the utility and probability of options be combined in the process of decision making?

12.   In what ways can heuristics lead to irrational judgments?

13.   What is meant by the expression "bounded rationality?"

14.   Explain how both learning and problem-solving can occur implicitly – that is, outside of awareness.

15.   How is "prospect theory" related to the way people assess risks?

16.   What is meant by the notions "parallel" and "distributed" in parallel distributed processing (PDP) models?

17.   Explain the process of parallel constraint satisfaction.

18.   Describe the consequences of damage to the dorsolateral and the ventromedial prefrontal cortex.

19.   What is the Whorfian hypothesis of linguistic relativity?

20.   How do morphemes differ from phonemes?

21.   How do listeners employ information about both syntax and semantics to understand the meaning of sentences?

22. How do people mentally represent discourse at multiple levels?

23 How is communication influenced by shared rules of conversation, as well as nonverbal communication?

24. How do behaviorists explain language acquisition? What challenges to this approach have been posed by the nativist position?

25. What evidence is there to support the notion of a critical period for language acquisition?

26. What are the differences between babbling and telegraphic speech?

27. How has research with chimps questioned the notion that language is unique to humans?

PART TWO: REVIEW AND LEARN
Key Terms, Fill-In Exercises, Application and Using What You Have Learned

Before doing the exercises below, review the information you learned in this chapter. Reread the work you did in part one of this study guide chapter, plus the interim summaries and end-of-chapter summary in your textbook. Review any problem areas. Once you feel comfortable with the material, do the following exercises without referring to your notes or textbook. If you have difficulty with a term or question, mark it and come back to it. When you have finished an exercise, go back to your notes and the textbook to find the answers to the questions that gave you difficulty. Finally, check your answers (key terms against the textbook and the rest against the answer key).

KEY TERMS

Upon completion of Chapter 7, you should be able to define the following terms.

Mental images _____

_____

Mental models _____

_____

Categories _____

_____

Defining features _____

_____

Concepts _____

_____

Categorization _____

_____

Well-defined concepts _____

_____

Fuzzy concepts _____

_____

Prototype _____

_____

Basic level _____

_____

Subordinate level _____

_____

Superordinate level _____

_____

Reasoning _____

_____

Inductive reasoning _____

_____

Deductive reasoning _____

_____

Syllogism _____

_____

Analogical reasoning _____

_____

Problem solving _____

_____

Well-defined problem _____

_____

Ill-defined problem _____

_____

Subgoals _____

_____

Problem-solving strategies   _____

_____

Algorithms   _____

_____

Mental simulation   _____

_____

Functional fixedness   _____

_____

Confirmation bias   _____

_____

Decision making   _____

_____

Weighted utility value   _____

_____

Expected utility   _____

_____

Explicit cognition   _____

_____

Heuristics   _____

_____

Representativeness heuristic   _____

_____

Availability heuristic _____

_____

Bounded rationality _____

_____

Implicit cognition _____

_____

Connectionism (or parallel distributed processing models)_____

_____

Constraint satisfaction _____

_____

Dorsolateral prefrontal cortex _____

_____

Ventromedial prefrontal cortex _____

_____

Language _____

_____

Whorfian hypothesis of liguistic relativity _____

_____

Phonemes _____

_____

Morphemes _____

_____

Phrases _____

_____

Sentences _____

_____

Syntax _____

_____

Grammar _____

_____

Semantics _____

_____

Pragmatics _____

_____

Discourse _____

_____

Nonverbal communication _____

_____

Universal grammar _____

_____

Language Acquisition Device (LAD) _____

_____

Babbling _____

_____

Telegraphic speech   _____

_____

FILL-IN EXERCISES

Fill in the word or words that best fit in the spaces below.

1.   _____ means manipulating mental representations for a purpose.

2.   _____ _____ are representations that describe, explain, or predict the way things work.

3.   The level that people naturally tend to use in categorizing objects is known as the _____ level. The level of categorization below this is the _____ level.

4.   _____ refers to the process by which people generate and evaluate arguments and beliefs.

5.   Reasoning that draws a conclusion from a set of assumptions or premises is referred to as _____ reasoning.

6.   The process by which people understand a novel situation in terms of a familiar one is referred to as _____ reasoning.

7.   In a well-defined problem, the _____ state, _____ state, and the _____ are easily determined.

8.   According to information-processing models, when people make decisions, they consider the _____ as well as the _____ of the outcomes of different options.

9.   The _____ heuristic assumes that events or occurrences that can be recalled easily must be common and are therefore likely to happen.

10.   "Aha" experiences, when people set aside a seemingly insoluble problem only to find hours or days later that the answer suddenly comes to them, are examples of _____ problem solving.

11.   Damage to the _____ prefrontal cortex can result in difficulty connecting feelings with thought, to make sound decisions.

12.   The Whorfian hypothesis of linguistic relativity holds that _____ shapes _____.

13.   The smallest units of sound that constitute speech are called _____, while the smallest units of meaning in a language are called _____.

14.   _____ refers to the rules that govern the placement of words and phrases in a sentence.

15. When parents provide feedback concerning their children's language, they focus less on _____ than on _____.

16. Short sentences in which children leave out all but the essential words are called _____ speech.

17. A _____ _____ refers to a point in development when the brain is maximally sensitive to language acquisition.

APPLICATION

For each of the following situations, identify the aspect of reasoning or problem solving that is illustrated.

1. Fred has taken his lucky rabbit's foot to the last three Dodgers' games, and they've won all three. He concludes that it's because of his rabbit's foot and vows to bring it to every game from now on. He remembers bringing it to the two other games he attended, and they won both times. He overlooks the fact that they've won almost every game at home this season, even though he's only been to five. What type of reasoning led Dave to his conclusion about the rabbit's foot? What type of bias is leading to Dave's erroneous conclusion?

2. When Nancy came over to Dave's for dinner, she was surprised that he was such a good cook. "Men can't cook," reasoned Nancy. "Dave is a man; therefore, Dave can't cook." What type of reasoning led Nancy to this conclusion?

3. Jane just can't forget the news report she saw on the big plane crash at the airport in her city. Ever since then, she won't fly anywhere. "Too much chance of a crash," Jane reasons. "Driving's much safer!" What led to this error in Jane's reasoning?

4. In screening new candidates for executive positions, Acme Tire company presents them with an Acme tire and asks them to come up with all possible uses for it that they can think of.

   "That's easy," says Geoff, a candidate for the position, "Put it on a car's wheels."
   The interviewer replies, "And what else could you use it for?"
   "On a truck's wheels," says Geoff, hesitatingly.
   "Anything else?" questions the interviewer.
   "I know!" says Geoff, proud of his ingenuity, "A trailer's wheels!"

   What limitation underlies Geoff's difficulty with the question?

USING WHAT YOU HAVE LEARNED

In Chapter 7 you read about how language and thought are interconnected. Many people find it hard even to consider problem solving without the use of language. In fact, some psychologists have stressed the role of self-directed communication in problem solving. Pay attention to your own problem-solving processes. Have you ever found yourself talking to yourself as you go through a problem step by step? Is it more likely to happen when you're all by yourself than with other people? Even if you don't talk out loud to yourself, do you ever talk to yourself "in your head?" Try to imagine thinking or problem solving without the use of language. Can you imagine what thinking might be like for a preverbal infant?

PART THREE: TEST AND KNOW
SAMPLE TEST QUESTIONS

Test how well you have learned this chapter's material by answering the sample test questions. You may wish to mark your answers on a separate sheet of paper so you can reuse this test for exam review. Once you have completed the exam, check your answers and then go back to your notes and the textbook to review questions you found difficult.

1.   A mental representation of a category (i.e, an internal portrait of a class of objects, ideas, or events that share common properties) is referred to as a

    a.   concept   b.   mental image
    c.   mental model   d.   prototype

2.   The concept "adult" is a good example of a(n)

    a.   prototype   b.   fuzzy concept
    c.   basic level category   d.   implicit category

3.   A prototype is

    a.   a visual representation, such as an image or a geometric form
    b.   a representation of a system that enables people to describe, explain, and predict how things work
    c.   a mental representation of a class of objects, ideas, or events that share common properties
    d.   an abstraction across many instances of a category

4.   Referring to robins, blue jays, and penguins as "animals" is an example of

    a.   the basic level of categorization
    b.   the superordinate level of categorization
    c.   the defining features method of categorization
    d.   the prototype-matching method of categorization

5. Bill has noticed that almost every time he shakes hands with someone who has a cold, he comes down with a cold, too. He concludes that the cold virus can be transmitted via hand-to-hand contact. This reasoning is an example of

   a. problem solving
   b. hypothesis testing
   c. inductive reasoning
   d. deductive reasoning

6. Your friend's mother claims that she was unable to program the VCR to record a favorite TV program until it was explained to her in terms of how she usually programs the microwave to cook a chicken while she is at work. This is an example of

   a. deductive reasoning
   b. analogical reasoning
   c. syllogistic reasoning
   d. inductive reasoning

7. Dave and Nancy sent out 100 invitations to their wedding. They then took the number of replies they received and multiplied them by the price per plate that the caterer had given, to arrive at the cost of the wedding reception dinner. This problem-solving strategy is an example of a(n)

   a. algorithm
   b. syllogism
   c. heuristic
   d. prototype

8. The process of weighing the pros and cons of different alternatives before making a choice is called

   a. critical thinking
   b. decision making
   c. inductive reasoning
   d. deductive reasoning

9. When the fan belt broke on her car, Melanie pulled out a pair of nylons from her shopping bag and told John "This will fix it!" John just couldn't see how you could use nylons for anything other than wearing. John's problem is known as

   a. the representativeness heuristic
   b. the availability heuristic
   c. the confirmation bias
   d. functional fixedness

10.   After spending the morning trying to solve a problem, Mazen decided to forget it. That night, while lying in bed, the answer suddenly came to him. This is an example of

    a.   implicit problem solving
    b.   reasoning by analogy
    c.   deductive reasoning
    d.   decision making

11.   Connectionist models differ from traditional information-processing models in that the underlying metaphor is no longer really "mind as computer." Rather it is mind as

    a.   a set of algorithms functioning in series
    b.   a set of heuristics involved in problem solving
    c.   a set of neurons that activate and inhibit one another
    d.   the programmer of the computer

12.   Damage to the _____ is associated with impaired planning, distractibility, and deficits in working memory.

    a.   dorsolateral prefrontal cortex
    b.   ventrolateral prefrontal cortex
    c.   ventromedial prefrontal cortex
    d.   dorsomedial prefrontal cortex

13.   The suffix "s," added to a noun to make it plural, is an example of

    a.   a phoneme
    b.   a constituent
    c.   a morpheme
    d.   transformational grammar

14.   The term _____ refers to the way language is used and understood in everyday life.

    a.   semantics   b.   pragmatics
    c.   universal grammar   d.   syntax

15.   Most English-speaking 4-year-olds use the reflexive pronoun "hisself" instead of the correct "himself." This tendency

    a.   is a clear example of the Whorfian theory of linguistic relativity
    b.   can be viewed as evidence of an innate set of neural structures for acquiring language
    c.   raises questions concerning the notion that there is a "critical period" for language acquisition
    d.   is evidence of how "motherese" affects language acquisition

16. The language development of children raised in extreme isolation

   a. provides evidence for the nonverbal communication hypothesis
   b. provides evidence for the behaviorist view of language acquisition
   c. typically surpasses that of non-isolated children because of the lack of distracters in their environment
   d. provides evidence for the critical period hypothesis

17. Chomsky argued that humans are born with what he called a _____ device, an innate set of neural structures for acquiring language.

   a. syntactical processing
   b. language processing
   c. grammatical awareness
   d. language acquisition

18. Nine-month-old Tammy frequently says "dada." This is an example of

   a. motherese
   b. telegraphic speech
   c. babbling
   d. fatherese

19. All of the following are characteristics of motherese, *except*

   a. fast rate of speech
   b. exaggerated intonation
   c. slow rate of speech
   d. high pitch

20. Twenty-month-old Danny points to the fridge and says, "Baby want milk." This is an example of

   a. babbling
   b. telegraphic speech
   c. the language acquisition device
   d. a syllogism

ANSWERS

FILL-IN EXERCISES

1. thinking 2. mental models 3. basic; subordinate 4. reasoning 5. deductive 6. analogical
7. initial; goal; operators 8. utility; probability 9. availability 10. implicit 11. ventromedial
12. language; thought 13. phonemes; morphemes 14. syntax 15. grammar; content 16. telegraphic
17. critical period

APPLICATION

1. inductive reasoning; confirmation bias
2. deductive reasoning (a syllogism)
3. availability heuristic
4. functional fixedness

SAMPLE TEST QUESTIONS

1.	a	11.	c
2.	b	12.	a
3.	d	13.	c
4.	b	14.	b
5.	c	15.	b
6.	b	16.	d
7.	a	17.	d
8.	b	18.	c
9.	d	19.	a
10.	a	20.	b

Chapter 8
Intelligence

PART ONE: PRE-READ AND WORK
Outline and Learning Objectives

Pre-read this chapter's table of contents and end-of-chapter summary. Then, use the outline segment-by-segment to help you work through the chapter. Jot down your own questions, comments, and notes in the space provided. Make a note of difficult areas that you will need to review (include page numbers). Then, answer the questions in the learning objectives section that follows. Check off those you are confident that you can answer well. Re-read the material in the text for the questions about which you are less confident. Record the important points from your reading in the space below each question.

OUTLINE

The Nature of Intelligence

Intelligence is Multifaceted and Functional

A Global Vista: The Cultural Context of Intelligence

Intelligence Testing

Binet's Scale

Intelligence Testing Crosses the Atlantic

One Step Further: The extremes of Intelligence

Validity and Limitations of IQ tests

Approaches to Intelligence

The Psychometric Approach

The Information-Processing Approach

A Theory of Multiple Intelligences

Heredity and Intelligence

From Brain to Behavior: Individual Differences in IQ

Group Differences: Race and Intelligence

Commentary: The Science and Politics of Intelligence

Central Questions: What is Intelligence and How Can We Measure It?

LEARNING OBJECTIVES

Upon completion of Chapter 8, you should be able to answer the following questions.

1.   What three questions are central to understanding intelligence?

2.   Explain how intelligence can be viewed as culturally defined.

3.   How did the efforts of Alfred Binet and those of Sir Francis Galton differ?

4.   What is meant by the concept of mental age, introduced by Binet and Simon in 1908?

5.   On the Stanford-Binet Scale (1916), how was an intelligence quotient (IQ score) calculated?

6.   What were David Wechsler's contributions to modern-day intelligence testing procedures?

7.   How is mental retardation defined, and what are some of its possible causes?

8.   What is "giftedness?"

9.   How can creativity be measured, and how is this attribute related to intelligence?

10.   Discuss the following criticisms and controversies that surround IQ testing: lack of a theoretical basis, possible cultural bias, questions of validity.

11.   What are Spearman's two factors, and how are they related to one another?

12.   How do fluid intelligence and crystallized intelligence differ?

13.   What are some of the limitations of the psychometric approach to intelligence?

14.   How would a cognitive psychologist, from the information-processing approach, define intelligence?

15.   What three processes underlie performance on intelligence tests, as identified by researchers studying cognitive processes?

16.   What is the major limitation of the information-processing approach to intelligence?

17.   What are the seven intelligences identified by Howard Gardner? What criteria did he employ in choosing them?

18.   What are the strengths and limitations of the theory of multiple intelligences?

19.   What do findings from twin, family, and adoption studies show about the influence of nature and nurture on intelligence?

20.   What has research shown concerning the issue of race and intelligence?

21.   Outline the three major conclusions of the American Psychological Association task force on intelligence and intelligence testing.

PART TWO: REVIEW AND LEARN
Key Terms, Fill-In Exercises, Application and Using What You Have Learned

Before doing the exercises below, review the information you learned in this chapter. Reread the work you did in part one of this study guide chapter, plus the interim summaries and end-of-chapter summary in your textbook. Review any problem areas. Once you feel comfortable with the material, do the following exercises without referring to your notes or textbook. If you have difficulty with a term or question, mark it and come back to it. When you have finished an exercise, go back to your notes and the textbook to find the answers to the questions that gave you difficulty. Finally, check your answers (key terms against the textbook and the rest against the answer key).

KEY TERMS

Upon completion of Chapter 8, you should be able to define the following terms.

Intelligence   _____

_____

Psychometric instruments   _____

_____

Intelligence tests   _____

_____

Mental age (MA)   _____

_____

Stanford-Binet scale   _____

_____

Intelligence quotient (IQ)_____

_____

Wechsler Adult Intelligence Scale-Third Edition (WAIS-III)_____

_____

Wechsler Intelligence Scale for Children-III (WISC-III)   _____

_____

Mental retardation   _____

_____

Giftedness   _____

_____

Creativity   _____

_____

Divergent thinking   _____

_____

Psychometric approach _____

_____

Factor analysis _____

_____

Two-factor theory of intelligence _____

_____

g-factor _____

_____

s-factors _____

_____

Gf-Gc theory _____

_____

Fluid intelligence _____

_____

Crystallized intelligence _____

_____

Knowledge base _____

_____

Theory of multiple intelligences _____

_____

FILL-IN EXERCISES

Fill in the word or words that best fit in the spaces below.

1.   In recent years, psychologists have come to recognize that intelligence is multi-_____, _____, and _____ defined.

2.   From a(n) _____ perspective, people use their intelligence to satisfy wishes and avoid things they fear.

3.   For the purpose of intelligence testing, psychologists use _____ instruments – tests that quantify psychological abilities such as intellectual ability – to see how people differ from and compare to each other on psychological "scales."

4.   The most direct ancestor of today's intelligence tests was developed in France, in the year 1905, by _____ _____.

5.   In addition to a single, overall IQ score, the WAIS-III yields separate scores for each of the 14 subtests and overall scores for _____ and _____ IQ.

6.   David Wechsler is credited with remedying the problems associated with the concept of *mental age* by abandoning the concept, and, instead, calculating IQ as an individual's position relative to peers of the same age on a _____ distribution.

7.   Roughly 2% of the American population is _____ _____, that is, significantly subaverage in general intellectual functioning, with deficits in adaptive behavior evident during childhood, and appear in more than one realm.

8.   _____ is a quality that is related to both intelligence and giftedness; this quality can be defined as "the ability to produce valued outcomes in a novel way."

9.   The _____ of a psychological test refers to its ability to assess the construct it was designed to measure.

10.   The primary tool of the psychometric approach to intelligence is _____ _____, a statistical procedure for identifying common elements that underlie performance across a set of tasks.

11.   Whereas _____ intelligence refers to people's store of knowledge, _____ intelligence refers to intellectual capacities that have no specific content but are used in processing information and approaching novel problems.

12.   According to the information-processing approach, intelligence is best defined as a _____ rather than as a measurable quantity; individual differences in intelligence are assumed to reflect differences in the _____ operations people use in thinking.

13.   Howard Gardner's theory of _____ intelligences firmly grounds intelligence in both its _____ and cultural context.

14.   The logic of _____, _____, and _____ studies, in distinguishing some of the influences of nature and nurture on intelligence, is to examine subjects whose genetic relatedness is known and to see whether or not degree of genetic relatedness predicts the size of the correlation between their IQs.

15.   The results of the Texas Adoption Project, like the findings of several other studies, suggest that although genes and environment both influence IQ in childhood, the impact of the family environment _____ (*increases/decreases*) with age, as the impact of genetics _____ (*increases/decreases*).

APPLICATION

1. A friend of yours has just watched a television talk show that focused on the IQ and race controversy. This is the first time your friend has ever heard about IQ differences between racial groups, and the whole issue has left her rather confused. Knowing that you're studying the topic of intelligence in your psychology course, she turns to you to provide answers to some of her questions. Her major question is whether intelligence is inherited or is the consequence of the environment in which a person grows up. Drawing on findings from twin, family, and adoption studies that you've read about in Chapter 8, what would you tell her concerning the relative roles of heredity and environment in both individual and group differences in IQ?

2. A friend who is a parent has just been told that her child has been identified as *"gifted."* She has lots of questions about what giftedness means. Because she knows that you've been studying the topic of intelligence, your friend asks what you can tell her about giftedness. She wonders whether giftedness is related to IQ. She's also heard, however, that giftedness has something to do with creativity and wonders how IQ and creativity may be related. Finally, she's heard stories that gifted children may grow up unhappy and socially maladjusted. From what you've read in Chapter 8, how would you answer her questions and concerns?

3. Two psychology students are discussing the criticism that IQ tests may be culturally biased. After examining sample questions from several popular IQ tests, they conclude that the biggest problem is questions that are heavily language-based and assess general knowledge. They propose developing a *"culture-free"* test that does not require language and does not assess general knowledge. Instead, their test would measure intelligence in terms of how quickly people can sort abstract geometrical shapes. They're convinced that their test couldn't possible be culturally biased. Based on what you've read in Chapter 8, do you agree? Why or why not?

USING WHAT YOU HAVE LEARNED

A senior in high school, Jeffrey almost didn't come to school today, at all. This morning his parents dropped a bombshell: They're getting a divorce! Coming as a complete shock, this news had a profound effect on Jeffrey, making him upset, confused, and sad. It's as if all of a sudden his whole world has been turned upside down. To make matters worse, today is the day that the Scholastic Aptitude Test (SAT) is being administered at Jeffrey's school. Being a straight A student, Jeffrey plans to attend college in the fall. His marks on the SAT will, to a large extent, influence whether or not he will be accepted into the college of his choice.

If you were a close friend of Jeffrey would you recommend that he write the SAT today? Why or why not? If Jeffrey decides to write the SAT, what effect might his present emotional state have on his test scores? If, during the test, Jeffrey is especially anxious to get home and talk things over with his parents, is this likely to make matters worse? Why or why not?

PART THREE: TEST AND KNOW
SAMPLE TEST QUESTIONS

Test how well you have learned this chapter's material by answering the sample test questions. You may wish to mark your answers on a separate sheet of paper so you can reuse this test for exam review. Once you have completed the exam, check your answers and then go back to your notes and the textbook to review questions you found difficult.

1.   Intelligence is functional. From an evolutionary perspective,

   a.   people use their intelligence to satisfy wishes and avoid things they fear.
   b.   intelligent behavior solves problems of adaptation and hence facilitates survival and reproduction.
   c.   intelligence is applied cognition, using cognitive skills to solve problems or obtain desired ends.
   d.   all of the above.

2.   Western views of intelligence typically emphasize:

   a.   verbal skills, and mathematical and spatial abilities
   b.   verbal skills, practical abilities, and competencies
   c.   personal qualities, skills, and cognitive style
   d   independence, alertness, and verbal skills

3.   History will remember _____, not only as the first to attempt to test mental abilities, but also as a pioneering statistician who discovered how to express the relationship between two variables using (the) _____ _____, a fundamental statistical tool for understanding intelligence and many other aspects of psychological functioning.

   a.   Galton; correlation coefficient   b.   Binet; correlation coefficient
   c.   Binet; factor analysis   d.   Spearman; factor analysis

4.   As proposed by Lewis Terman, which of the following formulas *correctly* expresses the intelligence quotient (IQ) as the relation between an individual's mental age (MA) and chronological age (CA) ?

   a.   IQ = (MA/CA) ? 100   b.   IQ = (CA/MA) ? 100
   c.   IQ = (MA/CA) X100   d.   IQ = (CA/MA) X100

5.   If the question "Who wrote Romeo and Juliet?" were asked as part of the WAIS-III, it would most likely be included as an item in the _____ subtest.

   a.   Vocabulary   b.   Performance
   c.   Comprehension   d.   Information

6.   As determined by intelligence tests, IQ is _____ related to school grades, showing a correlation coefficient of between _____ and _____.

a.   mildly; .60, .70   b.   strongly; .90, 1.0
c.   strongly; .60, .70   d.   mildly; .12, .20

7.   In the United States, approximately what percentage of mentally retarded individuals are classified as severely to profoundly retarded?

a.   2 %   b.   75 to 90%
c.   1% or less   d.   10%

8.   PKU

a.   is a highly heritable condition that can, however, be treated by dietary restrictions
b.   is a disorder most frequently caused by an extra chromosome
c.   frequently results from exposure of the fetus to alcohol early in pregnancy
d.   is often associated with poverty and other similar psychosocial causes

9.   In Western society, with its emphasis on academic aptitude as measured by psychometric tests, giftedness is most often equated with

a.   an IQ that is above average   b.   an IQ exceeding 130
c.   an IQ exceeding 200   d.   creativity

10.   One strategy for assessing creativity is to measure _____ thinking. This type of thinking involves generating multiple possibilities from a given situation, such as describing all the possible uses of a coffee cup.

a.   fluid   b.   functional
c.   divergent   d.   savant

11.   For many years, critics have argued that intelligence tests

a.   lack a theoretical basis
b.   fail to capture the type of practical intelligence involved in achieving goals in every day life
c.   are culturally biased
d.   all of the above

12.   IQ tests place individuals on a continuum of intelligence, but, in general, they do *not*

a.   provide an overall IQ score
b.   explain what intelligence is
c.   quantify intellectual functioning in a way that allows comparison among individuals
d.   predict school success

13.   Spearman's theory of intelligence

  a.   attempts to explain the specific cognitive processes that underlie intelligent behavior
  b.   dates back to 1857
  c.   distinguishes the g-factor, or general intelligence, from s-factors, or specific abilities
  d.   contends that highly intelligent people do not tend to be maladjusted

14.   The Gf-Gc theory distinguishes two general factors of _____ and _____ intelligence.

  a.   verbal; performance
  b.   fluid, crystallized
  c.   general; specific
  d.   all of the above

15.   In contrast to the psychometric approach, which tries to _____ basic abilities, the information-processing approach tries to understand the specific _____ that underlie intelligent behavior.

  a.   complicate; attitudes   b.   adapt; structure
  c.   quantify; processes   d.   none of the above

16.   Which of the following was *not* identified as a type of intelligence by Howard Gardner in his theory of multiple intelligences?

  a.   reasoning   b.   logical/mathematical
  c.   musical   d.   bodily/kinesthetic

17.   Which of the following three variables have been identified by information-processing theorists as being particularly important in explaining individual differences in intelligence?

  a.   speed of processing; memory strategies; socioeconomic status
  b.   knowledge base; cultural heritage; ability to acquire and apply mental strategies
  c.   memory strategies; socioeconomic status; divergent thinking patterns
  d.   speed of processing; knowledge base; ability to acquire and apply mental strategies

18.   Gardner argues that intelligences can be isolated based on a number of criteria, including

  a.   their neurological similarity, the presence of savants, and their similar courses of development
  b.   their neurological independence, the presence of savants, and their different courses of development
  c.   their neurological independence, the presence of savants, and their similar courses of development
  d.   their neurological similarity, the presence of savants, and their different courses of development

19. A longitudinal study examining the relation between a child's IQ at age 4 and 13 and the number of risk factors to which the child was exposed showed that:

   a. the child's IQ varied directly with the number of risk factors: the more risk factors, the higher the child's IQ

   b. the number of risk factors to which the child was exposed was unrelated to the child's IQ

   c. the child's IQ varied inversely with the number of risk factors: the more risk factors, the lower the child's IQ

   d. environmental variables have little or no effect on individual differences in intelligence

20. Which of the following is consistent with the conclusions of the American Psychological Association task force on intelligence and intelligence testing?

   a. The heritability of IQ is highest in children, but declines as people approach adulthood.

   b. IQ tests are highly predictive of school success

   c. IQ tests are biased against particular groups: they predict outcomes such as school performance between groups, but not within groups.

   d. all of the above

ANSWERS

FILL-IN EXERCISES

1. faceted; functional; culturally   2. psychodynamic   3. psychometric   4. Alfred Binet
5. verbal; performance   6. frequency   7. mentally retarded   8. creativity   9. validity
10. factor analysis   11. crystallized; fluid   12. process; cognitive   13. multiple; neurological
14. twin, family, adoption   15. decreases; increases

APPLICATION

1. Twin, family, and adoption studies show that *both* heredity and environment play important roles in influencing intelligence. While genetic factors may account for many of the observed individual differences in IQ, environmental factors likely account for differences between groups. The analogy of differences in the size of military uniforms from different eras helps explain these differences.

2. Giftedness is frequently defined as IQ exceeding 130, although common definitions extend to other forms of talent such as social, musical, or athletic ability. Creativity, a quality related to giftedness, is only moderately correlated with intelligence. Terman's research suggests that gifted individuals tend to have average or above-average adjustment, slightly better chances of marital success, and far greater likelihood of achieving vocational success than the general population.

3. The students are incorrect. Both sorting abstract geometric shapes and the emphasis on speed in their test can be culturally biased.

SAMPLE TEST QUESTIONS

1.	b	11.	d
2.	a	12.	b
3.	a	13.	c
4.	c	14.	b
5.	d	15.	c
6.	c	16.	a
7.	d	17.	d
8.	a	18.	b
9.	b	19.	c
10.	c	20.	b

Chapter 9
Consciousness

PART ONE: PRE-READ AND WORK
Outline and Learning Objectives

Pre-read this chapter's table of contents and end-of-chapter summary. Then, use the outline segment-by-segment to help you work through the chapter. Jot down your own questions, comments, and notes in the space provided. Make a note of difficult areas that you will need to review (include page numbers). Then, answer the questions in the learning objectives section that follows. Check off those you are confident that you can answer well. Re-read the material in the text for the questions about which you are less confident. Record the important points from your reading in the space below each question.

OUTLINE

The Nature of Consciousness

Functions of Consciousness

Consciousness and Attention

The Normal Flow of Consciousness

Perspectives on Consciousness

The Psychodynamic Unconscious

The Cognitive Unconscious

Commentary: An Integrated View of Consciousness

From Brain to Behavior: The Neuropsychology of Consciousness

Sleep and Dreaming

The Nature and Evolution of Sleep

Stages of Sleep

Three Views of Dreaming

Altered States of Consciousness

Meditation

Hypnosis

One Step Further: Is Hypnosis Real?

Drug-Induced States of Consciousness

A Global Vista: Religious Experiences in Cross-Cultural Perspective

Central Questions: Perspectives on Consciousness

LEARNING OBJECTIVES

Upon completion of Chapter 9, you should be able to answer the following questions.

1.   Discuss the two primary functions of consciousness -- monitor and control.

2.   Discuss the three functions (or components) of attention.

3.   How have researchers examine the phenomenon of divided attention?

4.   What is daydreaming?

5.   How are beeper studies used to investigate the flow of consciousness?

6.   What three mental systems comprise consciousness, according to Freud?

7.   What is subliminal perception? Can it be used to motivate consumer behavior?

8.   Can unconscious emotion and motivation influence behavior?

9.   How do cognitive psychologists view conscious and unconscious processes?

10.   What are blindsight and amnesia, and what insights do these disorders reveal concerning the neuropsychology of consciousness.

11.   What neural structures are involved in the experience of consciousness?

12.   What are "circadian rhythms," and how are they controlled? How are they related to the phenomenon of "jet lag?"

13.   What are the effects of extreme sleep deprivation?

14.   Describe each of the four stages of sleep.

15.   How do REM and NREM sleep differ?

16.   What are the similarities and differences in the psychodynamic, cognitive, and biological views of the nature and significance of dreaming?

17.   What is meant by the term "altered states of consciousness"?

18.   What are the characteristics of meditation?

19.   What are the characteristics of hypnosis?

20.   How did Ernest Hilgard discover the hidden observer, and what are the implications of this finding?

21.   Discuss the controversy over the use of hypnosis to retrieve forgotten memories.

22.   Is hypnosis real? Consider this question from two different perspectives: (a) that of a skeptic, and (b) that of an advocate of hypnosis.

23.   What are the effects of each of the following psychoactive substances?

        alcohol and other depressants

        stimulants

        hallucinogens

        marijuana

24.   In what ways might religious experiences be considered altered states of consciousness?

PART TWO: REVIEW AND LEARN
Key Terms, Fill-In Exercises, Application and Using What You Have Learned

Before doing the exercises below, review the information you learned in this chapter. Reread the work you did in part one of this study guide chapter, plus the interim summaries and end-of-chapter summary in your textbook. Review any problem areas. Once you feel comfortable with the material, do the following exercises without referring to your notes or textbook. If you have difficulty with a term or question, mark it and come back to it. When you have finished an exercise, go back to your notes and the textbook to find the answers to the questions that gave you difficulty. Finally, check your answers (key terms against the textbook and the rest against the answer key).

KEY TERMS

Upon completion of Chapter 9, you should be able to define the following terms.

States of consciousness _____

_____

Consciousness _____

_____

Attention_____

_____

Selective inattention   _____

_____

Divided attention_____

_____

Dichotic listening tasks   _____

_____

Daydreaming _____

_____

Experience sampling _____

_____

Beeper Studies _____

_____

Conscious mental processes _____

_____

Preconscious mental processes _____

_____

Unconscious mental processes _____

_____

Subliminal perception _____

_____

Cognitive unconscious _____

_____

Circadian rhythm _____

_____

Insomnia _____

_____

Rapid eye movement (REM) sleep _____

_____

Non-REM (N-REM) sleep _____

_____

Manifest content of a dream _____

_____

Latent content of a dream _____

_____

Altered states of consciousness _____

_____

Meditation _____

_____

Hypnosis _____

_____

Hypnotic susceptibility _____

_____

Hypermnesia _____

_____

Age regression _____

_____

Hypnotic analgesia _____

_____

Psychoactive substances _____

_____

Depressants   _____

_____

Stimulants   _____

_____

Hallucinations   _____

_____

Hallucinogens   _____

_____

Religious experiences   _____

_____

FILL-IN EXERCISES

Fill in the word or words that best fit in the spaces below.

1.   Two functions of consciousness are readily apparent: Consciousness _____ the self and the environment, and it _____ thought and behavior.

2.   _____ refers to the process of focusing conscious awareness, providing heightened sensitivity to a limited range of experience requiring more extensive information processing.

3.   Turning attention away from external stimuli to internal thoughts and imagined scenarios, referred to as _____, is a major component of the normal flow of consciousness.

4.   According to Freud unconscious processes are inaccessible to consciousness because they would be too anxiety provoking to acknowledge and hence are _____.

5.   Information-processing models often use the terms consciousness and _____ memory interchangeably.

6.   According to the cognitive perspective, _____ (*unconscious/preconscious*) cognitive processes refer to associations and schemas activated below the threshold of consciousness that influence conscious thought and behavior.

7.   Although people differ widely in the amount of sleep they need and the amount they actually get, most report sleeping _____ to _____ hours per night.

8.   A _____ rhythm is a cyclical, sleep-wake biological process.

9.   Researchers have recently discovered a modulatory neurotransmitter, called _____, that tends to foster sleep when an animal has been awake to long.

10.   Stage _____ sleep is marked by large, slow, rhythmic *delta* waves (less than 1 cycle per second). When delta waves comprise more than 50% of recorded brain activity, the person has entered Stage _____ sleep.

11.   Freud distinguished between the _____ content, or story line of a dream and the _____ content, or the dream's underlying meaning.

12.   Many religions, such as Buddhism, believe that _____ leads to a deepened understanding of reality.

13.   The limits of hypnosis are _____ *(significant/insignificant)* enough that many states in the United States now _____ *(outlaw/allow)* the use of hypnotically induced memories in court testimony.

14.   _____ _____ are drugs that operate on the nervous system to alter mental activity.

15.   Psychoactive substances alter consciousness not only _____, by facilitating or inhibiting neural transmission at the synapse, but also psychologically, through _____ beliefs and expectations.

16.   Contrary to what many people who rely on alcohol to elevate their mood believe, alcohol is actually a _____.

17.   Used since about 500 AD, _____ is one of the most *potent* pleasure-inducing substances, as well as one of the most addictive, ever discovered.

18.   Hallucinogenic drug use in Europe and North America dramatically increased in the 1960s with the discovery of the synthetic hallucinogen, _____.

USING WHAT YOU HAVE LEARNED

On the bus ride home from the state fair, you overhear a young couple in the seat in front of you talking about the "Amazing Alphonso," a hypnotist all of you have just watched perform. The woman is convinced that Alphonso and his show were a hoax; she's sure that most of his "volunteers" were really actors, planted in the audience. The rest, she contends, were just "going along," performing whatever bizarre behaviors Alphonso asked them to -- from barking like a dog to kissing all of the bald men in the audience on the head. As for herself, she's convinced she could *never* be hypnotized!

Having just read about altered states of consciousness, what information might you offer to this woman about the validity of hypnosis? How would you explain the concepts of hypnotic susceptibility and posthypnotic suggestion to her?

Hearing the discussion about the Amazing Alphonso, another passenger on the bus joins in the conversation. Right away, he's recognized as one of the volunteers from the audience who participated in the show! For the last hour, you've watched this man on stage, convinced he was a 6-year-old boy playing at the beach, as he painstakingly built a huge sand castle. When Alphonso walked up and kicked the sand castle over, the man actually cried! Although he is anxious to defend his experience as legitimate, the sand castle builder can remember very little about what went on. He says he was very relaxed, but that he wasn't really conscious of what he was doing. He even acts surprised when he is told about his own behavior and that of his fellow volunteers.

Does the sand castle builder's memory of having been hypnotized seem reasonable? Why or why not? What information might you offer to him about hypnosis? How would you explain the concepts of age regression and the hidden observer?

Now that you've established yourself as the "expert" on hypnosis (on this bus, at least), your fellow passengers want to hear more about what you know. What would you tell them about the use of hypnosis in retrieving forgotten memories? What about its use by police detectives to help solve cases? Finally, how would you summarize the controversy that has surrounded hypnosis?

APPLICATION

Situation

Over the last few weeks, a friend of yours has been having a terrible time getting a good night's sleep. She lies there for hours, unable to fall asleep, just watching the night pass by on the clock beside her bed. This situation has been going on for some time, and she's really starting to worry about it. Lately, she's been so worried about not getting a good night's sleep that she can hardly sleep at all.

Questions to Answer

1.   Based on what you've read about sleep, do you think your friend might be suffering from insomnia? What advice would you give her to cope with this condition?

2.   Determined to "sleep-in" on a rainy Saturday morning, your friend makes the decision that – regardless when she wakes up -- she will stay in bed, *no matter what*. Is this strategy likely to help her with her problem? Why or why not?

3.   In an effort to *exhaust* herself to sleep, your friend decides that she will attend a late-night high-impact aerobics class, then rush home and go to bed. Is this strategy likely to help her with her problem? Why or why not?

4.   When all else fails, your friend decides that she has no other alternative but to take some of her father's sleeping pills, in order to "put an end to this vicious cycle of sleeplessness, once and for all." What advice would you give her about this decision?

PART THREE: TEST AND KNOW
SAMPLE TEST QUESTIONS

Test how well you have learned this chapter's material by answering the sample test questions. You may wish to mark your answers on a separate sheet of paper so you can reuse this test for exam review. Once you have completed the exam, check your answers and then go back to your notes and the textbook to review questions you found difficult.

1.   Which of the following are able to respond to a stimulus at different levels of consciousness?

    a.   only amnesics
    b.   only individuals who have been hypnotized
    c.   all people
    d.   only individuals who have ingested psychoactive substances

2.   At any given time, people are dimly aware of

      a.   much more than what is conscious
      b.   only what is conscious
      c.   having certain painful memories repressed
      d.   preconscious and unconscious processes

3.   Splitting attention between two complex tasks is known as

      a.   split-brain attention   b.   dichotic attention
      c.   selective attention   d.   divided attention

4.   Alicia is participating in a research study. The experimenter has given her a difficult puzzle to solve; as Alicia works on the puzzle, she has been instructed to talk out loud, "simply reporting the contents of her consciousness." The experimenter records Alicia's verbalizations into categories, such as emotional tone, relevance to the task at hand, ways of solving the task, and so forth. This research is an example of the _____ technique.

      a.   normal flow   b.   subliminal priming
      c.   subliminal perception   d.   experience sampling

5.   Although consciousness occupied a central role in the first textbook on psychology, when _____ came into ascendance, the study of consciousness was relegated to the periphery of psychological awareness and remained that way until the 1980s

      a.   psychoanalysis
      b.   information-processing models
      c.   behaviorism
      d.   the evolutionary perspective

6.   As defined by Freud, _____ mental processes are not presently conscious, but could be readily brought to consciousness if the need arose.

      a.   subliminal   b.   preconscious
      c.   repressed   d.   unconscious

7.   Research into subliminal effects indicates that

      a.   the effects of subliminal messages are weak, cueing existing motives rather than creating new ones
      b.   certain types of subliminal messages -- especially backward messages in rock music -- may incite violence
      c.   subliminal messages are quite effective in motivating consumer behavior
      d.   subliminal messages are in many ways similar to posthypnotic suggestions, motivating people to actions they would not otherwise perform

8.   John Kihlstrom describes _____ cognitive processes as "skills or procedures that operate without awareness and are not accessible to consciousness under any circumstance."

   a.   unconscious   b.   preconscious
   c.   independent   d.   repressed

9.   Louise has no conscious visual awareness. When shown an object, she denies seeing it, yet she can indicate its location in space or describe its geometric form far better than one would expect simply by chance. Louise is likely suffering from

   a.   amnesia.   b.   blindsight.
   c.   split brain   d.   Korsakoff's disorder.

10.   Studies with amnesics have shown that people can remember things _____, even while lacking _____ memory.

   a.   over the long term; short-term
   b.   subliminally; long-term
   c.   under hypnosis; conscious
   d.   implicitly; explicit

11.   Which of the following *best* describes the relation between the number of hours that people sleep and mortality rates?

   a.   People who report sleeping for unusually short durations are prone to die earlier than are people who report sleeping eight to nine hours per night.
   b.   People who suffer from disorders of consciousness like blindsight, split brain, and amnesia are prone to die earlier than are people who report sleeping eight to nine hours per night.
   c.   People who report sleeping for unusually long *or* unusually short durations are prone to die earlier than those whose reported sleep is closer to average.
   d.   There is no relation between amount of sleep and mortality rates.

12.   When delta waves comprise more than 50 percent of recorded brain activity, a person has entered Stage _____ sleep.

   a.   1   b.   2
   c.   3   d.   4

13.   During a typical night's sleep, a complete cycle of REM and NREM sleep occurs about every _____.

   a.   90 minutes   b.   4 hours
   c.   30 minutes   d.   hour

14.   As proposed by _____, dreams express current concerns of one sort or another, in a language with its own peculiar grammar. For example, the thought, " I am worried about my upcoming exam," might be translated into a dream about falling off a cliff.

    a.   Freud   b.   Claparéde
    c.   Foulkes   d.   Kihlstrom

15.   People who are _____ tend to be able to form vivid visual images and to become readily absorbed in fantasy, daydreams, movies, and the like.

    a.   highly susceptible to subliminal messages
    b.   high in hypnotic susceptibility
    c.   quite able to develop a deep state of tranquility by altering their normal flow of conscious thoughts
    d.   highly susceptible to the effects of psychoactive substances

16.   Cross-culturally, the most widely used psychoactive substance is

    a.   LSD   b.   cocaine
    c.   alcohol   d.   marijuana

17.   In the United States, approximately one in _____ people abuse alcohol, and another one in _____ misuse other psychoactive substances.

    a.   five; seven   b.   seven; twenty
    c.   twenty; fifty   d.   ten; twenty

18.   Which of the following is *not* an example of a stimulant?

    a.   cocaine   b.   nicotine
    c.   amphetamines   d.   alcohol

19.   During a _____ high, judgment is moderately impaired, problem solving becomes less focused and efficient, and attention is more difficult to direct; some people also report paranoia or panic symptoms.

    a.   marijuana   b.   PCP
    c.   Xanax   d.   cocaine

20.   In _____, the soul is believed to be entered by another person or supernatural being.

    a.   meditation   b.   the "hidden observer" phenomenon
    c.   possession trances   d.   an LSD high

ANSWERS

FILL-IN EXERCISES

1. monitors; controls   2. attention   3. daydreaming   4. repressed   5. working
6. preconscious   7. 6.5; 8.5   8. circadian   9. adenosine   10. three; four
11. manifest; latent   12. meditation   13. significant; outlaw   14. psychoactive substances
15. physiologically; cultural   16. depressant   17. cocaine   18. lysergic acid diethylamide (LSD)

APPLICATION

1. Yes. This certainly sounds like insomnia. She should establish a regular sleep schedule, avoid activities that will produce autonomic nervous system arousal before bedtime, and if she cannot sleep, get up, rather than roll around endlessly in bed. She should get rid of the clock beside the bed!

2. No, this is not likely to help. The bed becomes a conditioned stimulus for anxiety resulting from not sleeping, which feeds the insomnia.

3. No, this is not likely to help. This will increase autonomic nervous system arousal and may aggravate the problem.

4. This could aggravate the problem. She might become dependent on them as the brain develops a tolerance, requiring higher doses.

SAMPLE TEST QUESTIONS

1.	c	11.	c
2.	a	12.	d
3.	d	13.	a
4.	d	14.	c
5.	c	15.	b
6.	b	16.	c
7.	a	17.	b
8.	a	18.	d
9.	b	19.	a
10.	d	20.	c

Chapter 10
Motivation

PART ONE: PRE-READ AND WORK
Outline and Learning Objectives

Pre-read this chapter's table of contents and end-of-chapter summary. Then, use the outline segment-by-segment to help you work through the chapter. Jot down your own questions, comments, and notes in the space provided. Make a note of difficult areas that you will need to review (include page numbers). Then, answer the questions in the learning objectives section that follows. Check off those you are confident that you can answer well. Re-read the material in the text for the questions about which you are less confident. Record the important points from your reading in the space below each question.

OUTLINE

Perspectives on Motivation

Evolutionary Perspective

Psychodynamic Perspective

Behaviorist Perspective

Cognitive Perspective

A Hierarchy of Needs

Applying the Perspectives on Motivation

A Global Vista: Cultural Influences on Motivation

Eating

Homeostasis

What Turns Hunger On?

What Turns Hunger Off?

Obesity

Sexual Motivation

The Sexual Response Cycle

Sexual Orientation

From Brain to Behavior: The Biology of Homosexuality

Psychosocial Motives

Needs for Relatedness

Achievement and Other Agency Motives

Central Questions: The Nature and Causes of Human Motives

LEARNING OBJECTIVES

Upon completion of Chapter 10, you should be able to answer the following questions.

1. How does the theory of inclusive fitness account for the motivation to care for close relatives?

2. What are pheromones and what role do they play in communication between organisms?

3. What two basic drives, according to Freud, motivate human behavior?

4. How do current psychodynamic views of motivation differ from Freud's view?

5. How do implicit motives and explicit motives differ?

6. How are secondary drives acquired and how do they differ from primary drives, according to the behaviorist perspective?

7.   How do goals serve as motivational variables, according to the cognitive perspective?

8.   Outline six conditions necessary for maximum job performance, according to goal-setting theory.

9.   What are three innate needs suggested by self-determination theory, and how does this theory view the effects of reward?

10.   What are Maslow's five categories of needs and how are they organized?

11.   Describe the three levels of needs that form the basis of ERG theory.

12.   How can culture shape motivation?

13.   What are the two phases of metabolism?

14.   In what ways can the system that regulates food intake be considered a homeostatic system?

15.   How is the experience of being overweight influenced by gender and culture?

16.   What are two physiological factors that seem especially important in creating obesity?

17.   What role may environmental and psychological factors play in obesity?

18.　　Outline the four phases of the sexual response cycle.

19.　　What insight do androgen insensitivity syndrome and congenital adrenal hyperplasia provide into the organizational role of sex hormones?

20.　　Describe the research suggesting a biological basis for homosexuality.

21.　　Why are needs for relatedness -- such as attachment, intimacy, and affiliation -- important?

22.　　How do people with a high need for achievement characteristically behave?

23.　　How do performance goals and mastery goals differ?

24.　　How is need for achievement related to both parental and cultural expectations?

PART TWO:　REVIEW AND LEARN
Key Terms, Fill-In Exercises, Application and Using What You Have Learned

Before doing the exercises below, review the information you learned in this chapter. Reread the work you did in part one of this study guide chapter, plus the interim summaries and end-of-chapter summary in your textbook. Review any problem areas. Once you feel comfortable with the material, do the following exercises without referring to your notes or textbook. If you have difficulty with a term or question, mark it and come back to it. When you have finished an exercise, go back to your notes and the textbook to find the answers to the questions that gave you difficulty. Finally, check your answers (key terms against the textbook and the rest against the answer key).

KEY TERMS

Upon completion of Chapter 10, you should be able to define the following terms.

Motivation _____

_____

Instincts _____

_____

Drives _____

_____

Thematic Apperception Test (TAT) _____

_____

Drive reduction theories _____

_____

Primary drive _____

_____

Secondary drive _____

_____

Incentive _____

_____

Goals _____

_____

Goal-setting theory _____

_____

Intrinsic motivation   _____

_____

Self-determination theory   _____

_____

Implicit motives   _____

_____

Expectancy-value theories   _____

_____

Hierarchy of needs   _____

_____

Self-actualization needs   _____

_____

ERG theory   _____

_____

Metabolism   _____

_____

Absorptive phase   _____

_____

Fasting phase   _____

_____

Homeostasis   _____

_____

Set point _____

_____

Feedback mechanisms _____

_____

Corrective mechanisms _____

_____

Satiety mechanisms _____

_____

Obesity _____

_____

Set-point theory _____

_____

Sexual response cycle _____

_____

Organizational effects _____

_____

Androgen insensitivity syndrome _____

_____

Congenital adrenal hyperplasia _____

_____

Activational effects _____

_____

Sexual orientation _____

_____

Psychosocial needs _____

_____

Relatedness _____

_____

Agency _____

_____

Attachment motivation _____

_____

Intimacy _____

_____

Affiliation _____

_____

Need for achievement _____

_____

Performance goals _____

_____

Performance-approach goals _____

_____

Performance-avoidance goals _____

_____

Mastery goals _____

_____

FILL-IN EXERCISES

Fill in the word or words that best fit in the spaces below.

1.   Motivation has two components: _____ people want to do (the goals they pursue) and _____ they want to do it.

2.   _____ are relatively fixed patterns of behavior that animals produce without learning.

3.   Freud proposed that the two basic drives underlying human behavior are _____ and _____. Contemporary psychodynamic theorists, however, emphasize two other motives: the need for _____ to others and the need for _____-_____.

4.   Many contemporary psychodynamic theorists have moved away from Freud's abstract notion of "drives" to two concepts that seem closer to the data of clinical observation: _____ and _____ .

5.   The Thematic Apperception Test (TAT) taps _____ motives, whereas self-reports reflect _____ motives.

6.   According to the behaviorist view, unfulfilled needs lead to _____, defined as states of arousal that motivate behavior.

7.   Cognitive researchers often focus on _____ (desired outcomes established through social learning) as a motivational construct.

8.   A cognitive theory of motivation used widely by organizational psychologists interested in worker motivation is goal-_____ theory.

9.   Abraham Maslow proposed that needs are organized according to a _____.

10.   _____ needs represent the most basic level of needs, according to Maslow.

11.   ERG theory condenses the needs described by Maslow to the following three levels: _____, _____, and _____.

12.   Erich Fromm argued that a culture's socioeconomic system shapes people's motivations so that they _____ to act in ways that the system _____ them to act.

13.   _____ refers to the body's tendency to maintain a relatively constant state that permits cells to live and function.

14. Like other homeostatic systems, the system regulating food intake includes several features. First, it has a _____ _____, a biologically optimal level that it strives to maintain. Second, it must have _____ mechanisms that provide it with information regarding the state of the system. Finally, it must have _____ mechanisms to restore it to its biologically optimal level when needed.

15. Obesity is defined as body weight that is _____ % or more above the ideal for one's height and age.

16. _____-_____ theory suggests that each person has a natural weight to which his or her body gravitates.

17. During the _____ phase of the sexual response cycle, the person's physiological and psychological functioning gradually returns to normal.

18. In contemporary Western society, approximately _____ to _____ % of men and _____ % of women consider themselves homosexual.

19. Two major clusters of psychosocial goals pursued cross-culturally are _____ (or communion) and _____ (motives for achievement, autonomy, mastery, power, and other self-oriented goals).

20. The need for _____ -- to do well, to succeed, and to avoid failure -- is the _____ (*best/least*) researched psychosocial motive.

USING WHAT YOU HAVE LEARNED

For some time, it has been known that cigarette smoking is linked to a host of serious medical problems, including increased risk of cardiac problems, emphysema, circulatory problems, and especially lung cancer. The risks inherent in smoking are well-publicized. There are anti-smoking ads on TV and in other media. As well, speakers address teenagers in high school, exhorting them not to begin smoking or, if they already have, to quit smoking. The percentage of the population that smokes has declined significantly. Yet many teenagers still take up smoking. In fact, there has been an increase lately in the number of teenage girls who take up smoking.

A national committee has been formed to investigate the causes of teenage smoking. You have been appointed to the committee, because it is well known that you are able to understand motivation from multiple perspectives. The committee turns to you for a brief report on what might underlie the apparently self-destructive behavior of teenagers who take up smoking. They want to attack this problem from as many angles as possible and ask you to "cover all the bases," theoretically. Referring to as many perspectives as possible, how would you explain people continuing to smoke, despite the risk? What suggestions would you offer to deal with this problem?

APPLICATION

Situation

Two of your friends are engaged in a heated discussion about obesity. One argues that obesity is the biggest preventable health problem after smoking. She believes that obese people need to use only a little self-control and reduce their calorie intake to control their weight problem. The other student agrees and adds that, as far as she's concerned, the "majority" of women are overweight. The two students agree and go on to talk about how "lazy," unattractive, and socially inept overweight people are.

Having just studied the topic of motivation, you feel you are in a position to offer some informed input. Based on what you have read, address the following points.

Questions to Answer

1.   To what extent is obesity a health problem?

2.   Is it true that the majority of women are overweight? What is the medical definition of obesity? Approximately what proportion of the adult American population is obese?

3.   Could the student's view that the "majority" of women are overweight be culturally biased? How would someone have responded in an earlier time or perhaps in a non-western culture?

4.   How would you respond to the students' statements about the laziness, attractiveness, and social skills of overweight people?

5.   Is it true that all that's needed is willpower and dieting? How could you explain to these students that the issue is more complicated than they think (Hint: refer to set-point theory.)

PART THREE: TEST AND KNOW
SAMPLE TEST QUESTIONS

Test how well you have learned this chapter's material by answering the sample test questions. You may wish to mark your answers on a separate sheet of paper so you can reuse this test for exam review. Once you have completed the exam, check your answers and then go back to your notes and the textbook to review questions you found difficult.

1.   The primary motivations that emerge in cross-cultural research are

   a.   power; love   b.   relatedness to others; self-esteem
   c.   sex; aggression   d.   achievement; intimacy

2. In addition to sexual and aggressive desires, current psychodynamic theorists emphasize two other motives:

   a. power; love
   b. relatedness to others; self-esteem
   c. sex; aggression
   d. achievement; intimacy

3. Which of the following can be considered a secondary drive?

   a. the desire for food
   b. the desire for water
   c. the desire for money
   d. the desire for sex

4. Self-determination theory suggests that people have three innate needs:

   a. existence, belongingness, goals
   b. physiological needs, safety needs, belongingness needs
   c. attachment, sex, aggression
   d. competence, autonomy, relatedness to others

5. At the highest level in Maslow's hierarchy of needs are

   a. self-actualization needs
   b. safety needs
   c. belongingness needs
   d. esteem needs

6. Self-actualization needs differ from other needs in Maslow's hierarchy in that they are

   a. deficiency needs
   b. esteem needs
   c. belongingness needs
   d. growth needs

7. ERG theory condenses Maslow's hierarchy to three levels:

   a. esteem, relatedness, growth
   b. existence, reproduction, growth
   c. existence, resolution, growth
   d. existence, relatedness, growth

8. The absorptive phase and fasting phase are the two phases of

   a. the sexual response cycle
   b. homeostasis
   c. metabolism
   d. palatability

9.   Mechanisms for "turning off" ingestive behavior are known as

    a.   satiety mechanisms
    b.   corrective mechanisms
    c.   feedback mechanisms
    d.   set point mechanisms

10.   Many dieters find that the more weight they lose, the harder losing becomes. This is likely because as weight drops, so, too, does metabolic level. Which of the following best explains this phenomenon?

    a.   the functioning of *neuropeptide y* in the hypothalamus
    b.   satiety mechanisms
    c.   corrective mechanisms
    d.   set-point theory

11.   Maximum arousal occurs during which phase of the sexual response cycle?

    a.   resolution
    b.   plateau
    c.   orgasm
    d.   excitement

12.   The final phase of the sexual response cycle is

    a.   resolution
    b.   orgasm
    c.   plateau
    d.   excitement

13.   A disorder in which the adrenal glands secrete too much androgen in utero, masculinizing the genitals in females, is

    a.   congenital adrenal hyperplasia
    b.   androgen insensitivity syndrome
    c.   maternal stress syndrome
    d.   anorexia nervosa

14.   Unless hormones called _____ are present, human fetuses will automatically develop into _____.

    a.   estrogens; males
    b.   androgens; males
    c.   androgens; females
    d.   estrogens; females

15. The direction of a person's enduring sexual attraction is referred to as

    a.   sexual preference
    b.   sexual response
    c.   sexual orientation
    d.   sexual motivation

16. The desire for physical and psychological proximity to another person is called

    a.   attachment motivation
    b.   the first phase of the sexual response cycle
    c.   sexual attraction
    d.   affiliation motivation

17. Women who report having _____ are 10 times less likely to suffer depression following a stressful event than women who do not.

    a.   a confidante
    b.   an active sexual life
    c.   a rewarding career
    d.   money

18. People high in need for achievement

    a.   enjoy being challenged and are not worried about failing
    b.   worry so much about failure that they will only undertake tasks if they are assured of success
    c.   tend to take risks because of their insatiable need for challenge
    d.   enjoy being challenged but do not want to fail

19. Bill is studying photography. He's not doing it to get the diploma that comes at the end of his program. Rather, his primary purpose is to become a better photographer. His goal would be described as a

    a.   performance goal
    b.   performance-avoidance goal
    c.   mastery-avoidance goal
    d.   mastery goal

20. Which of the following parenting practices is *not* associated with a high need for achievement?

    a.   discouraging children from complaining
    b.   encouraging children to attempt new tasks well beyond their reach
    c.   encouraging independent thinking
    d.   prompting children to try new solutions when they encounter failure

ANSWERS

FILL-IN EXERCISES

1. what; how strongly   2. instincts   3. sex, aggression; relatedness, self-esteem   4. wishes; fears
5. implicit (unconscious); explicit (conscious)   6. drives   7. goals   8. setting   9. hierarchy   10. physiological
11. existence, relatedness, growth   12. want; needs   13. homeostasis   14. set point; feedback; corrective
15. 15   16. set-point   17. resolution   18. 2; 7; 1   19. relatedness; agency   20. achievement; best

APPLICATION

1. Obesity is associated with heart disease, high blood pressure, diabetes, and an increased mortality rate.

2. The majority is not overweight, although the percentage is increasing. Body weight that is 15% above the ideal for one's height and age is the definition of obesity. By this criterion, approximately 1/3 of the population in the United states is obese.

3. Yes, their view could be culturally biased. White, North American culture is preoccupied with thinness. Standards in other cultures or other eras are (were) different. Beauty is associated with bulk in many other cultures.

4. These are stereotypes that can lead to differences in how obese people are treated, which can result lowered self-esteem and negative expectations about how others will treat you.

5. Each person has a natural weight to which the body gravitates, regulated by the hypothalamus. If a person lowers his or her caloric input through dieting, the body may slow metabolism to maintain the set-point weight in spite of fewer calories. Thus, the more you lose, the harder losing may become.

SAMPLE TEST QUESTIONS

1.	a		11.	b
2.	b		12.	a
3.	c		13.	a
4.	d		14.	c
5.	a		15.	c
6.	d		16.	a
7.	d		17.	a
8.	c		18.	d
9.	a		19.	d
10.	d		20.	b

Chapter 11
Emotion, Stress, and Coping

PART ONE: PRE-READ AND WORK
Outline and Learning Objectives

Pre-read this chapter's table of contents and end-of-chapter summary. Then, use the outline segment-by-segment to help you work through the chapter. Jot down your own questions, comments, and notes in the space provided. Make a note of difficult areas that you will need to review (include page numbers). Then, answer the questions in the learning objectives section that follows. Check off those you are confident that you can answer well. Re-read the material in the text for the questions about which you are less confident. Record the important points from your reading in the space below each question.

OUTLINE

Emotion

Physiological Components

Subjective Experience

Emotional Expression

A Taxonomy of Emotions

From Brain to Behavior: The Neuropsychology of Emotion

Emotion Regulation

Perspectives on Emotion

Stress

Stress as a Psychobiological Process

Stress as a Transactional Process

Sources of Stress

Stress and Health

Coping

Coping Mechanisms

A Global Vista: The Impact of Culture on Coping Styles

Social Support

Central Questions: Thinking about Feeling

LEARNING OBJECTIVES

Upon completion of Chapter 11, you should be able to answer the following questions.

1. What are the differences in how the James-Lange theory and the Cannon-Bard theory account for emotional experiences?

2. How does emotional disclosure affect health?

3. Can facial expressions actually influence a person's emotional state? How?

4. What are the six facial expressions recognized by people of most cultures?

5. What are *display rules* and how are they culturally relevant?

6. What are the differences in how men and women experience and express emotion?

7. How are positive and negative affect related to approach and avoidance?

8.   Describe a hierarchical system for classifying emotions.

9.   What are the roles of the hypothalamus, limbic system, and cortex in emotion?

10.   What are the physiological mechanisms underlying two stages of emotional reaction in humans?

11.   What is meant by *emotion regulation*? What are some common emotion regulation strategies that people use?

12.   What have researchers found concerning the influence of unconscious emotional processes?

13.   According to the Schacter-Singer theory of emotion, how do physiological arousal and cognitive interpretation interact?

14.   What role does appraisal play in people's emotional responding?

15.   Can mood influence the encoding and retrieval of information? How?

16.   What differences exist between males and females in terms of jealousy, according to the evolutionary perspective?

17.   In what ways can stress be considered both a psychobiological and a transactional process?

18.   What are the three stages of the *general adaptation syndrome*?

19.   What are the differences between *primary appraisal* and *secondary appraisal* according to Richard Lazarus's model of stress and coping?

20.   How are life events, catastrophes, and daily hassles sources of stress? What are the possible effects of each?

21.   How does stress affect the body's capacity to fight illness?

22.   What is the Type-A behavior pattern and how is it related to health problems?

23.   Is optimism/pessimism related to health? How?

24.   How do *problem-focused* strategies for coping with stress and *emotion-focused* strategies differ?

25.   Explain the differences between *low-effort syndrome* and *John Henryism*.

26.   What are two explanations for the beneficial effects of social support in coping with stress?

PART TWO: REVIEW AND LEARN
Key Terms, Fill-In Exercises, Application and Using What You Have Learned

Before doing the exercises below, review the information you learned in this chapter. Reread the work you did in part one of this study guide chapter, plus the interim summaries and end-of-chapter summary in your textbook. Review any problem areas. Once you feel comfortable with the material, do the following exercises without referring to your notes or textbook. If you have difficulty with a term or question, mark it and come back to it. When you have finished an exercise, go back to your notes and the textbook to find the answers to the questions that gave you difficulty. Finally, check your answers (key terms against the textbook and the rest against the answer key).

KEY TERMS

Upon completion of Chapter 11, you should be able to define the following terms.

Emotional forecasting _____

_____

Emotion (or affect) _____

_____

James-Lange theory _____

_____

Cannon-Bard theory _____

_____

Emotional expression _____

_____

Display rules _____

_____

Basic emotions _____

_____

Positive affect _____

_____

Negative affect _____

_____

Emotion regulation (or affect regulation) _____

_____

Moods _____

_____

Attributions _____

_____

Schachter-Singer theory _____

_____

Stress _____

_____

General adaptation syndrome _____

_____

Primary appraisal _____

_____

Secondary appraisal _____

_____

Stressors _____

_____

Acculturative stress _____

_____

Catastrophes _____

_____

Daily hassles _____

_____

Immune system _____

_____

Antibodies _____

_____

Type A behavior pattern _____

_____

Coping _____

_____

Low effort syndrome _____

_____

John Henryism _____

_____

Social support _____

_____

FILL-IN EXERCISES

Fill in the word or words that best fit in the spaces below.

1. William James's approach to emotion is also called the _____ theory of emotion.

2. According to the _____-_____ theory, emotion-inducing stimuli simultaneously elicit both an emotional experience and bodily responses.

3. Evidence suggests that _____ *(men/women)* are able to read emotions from other people's faces and nonverbal cues better than _____ *(men/women)*.

4. Patterns of emotional expression considered appropriate within a culture or subculture are referred to as _____ _____.

5. An emotion is referred to as _____ if it has characteristic physiological, subjective, and expressive components.

6. Approach-oriented feelings and motives are processed to a greater extent in the _____ *(right/left)* frontal cortex, whereas avoidance-oriented feelings and motives are associated with the _____ *(right/left)* frontal cortex.

7. The term _____ refers to relatively enduring emotional states that can provide a background sense of positive or negative well-being.

8. According to the _____-_____ theory, emotion involves two factors: physiological arousal and cognitive interpretation. Research shows, however, that while _____ may intensify emotional experience, it may not be necessary for an emotion to occur.

9. According to Robert Zajonc, people become more positive about a stimulus the more times it is displayed to them, a phenomenon referred to as the *mere* _____ *effect*.

10. Stress can be considered both a _____ process and a _____ process.

11. The organism is especially vulnerable to illness in the _____ stage of the general adaptation syndrome.

12. According to Lazarus's model of stress and coping, in the _____ appraisal stage, the person decides whether the situation is benign, stressful, or irrelevant.

13. Change is one of the most significant sources of _____.

14. _____ stress refers to the stress that people experience when trying to adapt to a new culture.

15. Stressors of massive proportion are referred to as _____.

16.   In the immune system, B cells produce _____, protein molecules that attach themselves to foreign invaders and mark them for destruction.

17.   Individuals who are impatient, hard-driving, ambitious, competitive, and hostile display what is called the _____ behavior pattern.

18.   Coping mechanisms aimed at changed the stressful situation are called _____-focused. Efforts to alter one's thoughts about the situation, or to alter the unpleasant affective consequences of stress, are called _____-focused.

USING WHAT YOU HAVE LEARNED

How's Your Stress?

One of the sources of stress you read about in Chapter 11 was life events. Consider the stressful life events you have confronted over the past 12 months. Have you experienced any major stressors? Have you had to deal with more than one stressful life event? Can you see how their effects can add up?

How many of the stressors you're dealing with can be considered "challenges," that is, positive changes in your life? Can you see how even positive life events can be considered stressors?

What are some of the "daily hassles" you deal with? Is it apparent to you how they can be considered sources of stress?

How do you deal with stress? Do you use physical exercise or relaxation? How about social support? Are you able to talk to another person or people about the life events you're dealing with?

What would you say are the most common stressors that university students have to cope with?

APPLICATION

Situation

Two students in your psychology class are having a heated debate about how thinking and feeling are related. One argues that how she feels affects what she thinks. She says that when she's feeling down, everything looks negative, while on days when she's feeling really happy, she can hardly even remember negative things. The other student agrees that thinking and feeling are related, but argues that it's thinking that affects feeling, and not the other way around. She argues that it's how her friend interprets the situation that leads to feeling down or really happy. Who's right?

Questions to Answer

1.   With reference to the various perspectives on emotion covered in the chapter, discuss how emotion and cognition are related.

2.   Try for yourself to see how cognition and emotion are related. Pay attention to your thoughts and attributions when your mood changes. Does your mood affect your thoughts? Can you influence your emotional state by changing the content of your cognitions?

3.   What role might the physiological components of emotion play in the relation between emotion and cognition?

4.   What role does cognition play in people's emotional reaction to stressful situations? Is there a role for cognition in the coping process?

PART THREE: TEST AND KNOW
SAMPLE TEST QUESTIONS

Test how well you have learned this chapter's material by answering the sample test questions. You may wish to mark your answers on a separate sheet of paper so you can reuse this test for exam review. Once you have completed the exam, check your answers and then go back to your notes and the textbook to review questions you found difficult.

1.   The James-Lange theory of emotion sees the origins of emotion in

    a.   the peripheral nervous system
    b.   the cognitive appraisal of the stressfulness of an event
    c.   the attributions people make concerning their ability to cope
    d.   how we encode and retrieve information about an experience

2.   The correlation between self-reported happiness and economic prosperity

    a.   is actually negative; money and happiness are inversely related
    b.   is insignificant, regardless of culture or situation
    c.   is substantial within cultures, although minimal across cultures
    d.   is substantial across cultures, although minimal within cultures

3.   In addition to indicating a person's emotional state, facial expressions

    a.   indicate how well she's coping with stress
    b.   tell you what she's thinking
    c.   can indicate what coping mechanisms she's using
    d.   can influence patterns of autonomic response

4.   Cross cultural studies have identified six facial expressions recognized by people of all cultures. These are

    a.   surprise, fear, anger, disgust, happiness, sadness
    b.   anger, fear, curiosity, sadness, contempt, love
    c.   fear, trust, anticipation, love, hate, curiosity
    d.   guilt, shame, fear, anger, joy, friendliness

5.   Even children as young as 3 years old recognize that males are more likely than females to express the emotion _____.

    a.   fear
    b.   anger
    c.   happiness
    d.   sadness

6.   Positive and negative affect are regulated by different neurotransmitter systems. For example, people who are "fear driven" are hypothesized to have an abundance of or greater reaction to

a.   dopamine
b.   serotonin
c.   norepinephrine
d.   endorphins

7.   One emotion that does not fit neatly into the fundamental distinction between positive and negative affect is

a.   fear
b.   happiness
c.   trust
d.   anger

8.   Probably the most important limbic structure for emotion is the

a.   hypothalamus
b.   cerebellum
c.   thalamus
d.   amygdala

9.   The notion that a cognitive judgment or attribution is crucial to emotional experience is central to which theory of emotions?

a.   James-Lange
b.   Cannon-Bard
c.   Schachter-Singer
d.   Robert Zajonc's

10.   The finding that people more readily recall positive information when in a positive mood illustrates that

a.   positive information is much easier to encode than negative information
b.   negative information is much harder to recall than positive information
c.   emotional states influence both encoding and recall of information in memory
d.   both a and b

11.   According to the evolutionary perspective, jealousy in males should focus on

a.   the female's emotional commitment to other males
b.   the female's emotional commitment to other females
c.   the female's sexual relations with other males
d.   the male's access to the female's resources

12.   The three stages of the general adaptation syndrome, by which the body reacts to stress, include

    a.   alarm, appraisal, coping
    b.   alarm, fleeing, fighting
    c.   alarm, plateau, recovery
    d.   alarm, resistance, exhaustion

13.   During the alarm stage of the general adaptation syndrome

    a.   the organism is especially vulnerable to illness
    b.   the body eventually wears down, if the phase lasts long enough
    c.   adrenaline and other hormones are released and the sympathetic nervous system is activated
    d.   all systems may appear to have returned to normal, although the body continues to use its resources at an accelerated rate

14.   According to Richard Lazarus, stress and coping involve two stages. The stage in which a person evaluates his or her options and determines how to respond is referred to as the

    a.   coping stage
    b.   resistance stage
    c.   primary appraisal stage
    d.   secondary appraisal stage

15.   Richard Lazarus distinguishes three types of stress:

    a.   challenge, threat, catastrophes
    b.   harm or loss, threat, challenge
    c.   exhaustion, harm or loss, catastrophes
    d.   hassles, catastrophes, life events

16.   The most stressful of life events, according to the Holmes-Rahe Life Events Rating Scale is

    a.   being fired at work
    b.   death of a spouse
    c.   divorce
    d.   being jailed

17.   Daily hassles

    a.   in contrast to life events are unlikely to serve as stressors
    b.   not only influence, but can also reflect the quality of interpersonal relationships
    c.   can easily be coped with by using a little denial
    d.   are stressful only for individuals displaying the Type-A behavior pattern

18.   The Type-A characteristic that is particularly related to heart disease is

    a.   hostility
    b.   competitiveness
    c.   impatience
    d.   ambitiousness

19.   John Henryism is a coping style characterized by

    a.   a tendency to work hard and cope actively despite difficult circumstances
    b.   the tendency to exert minimal effort to escape stressful social and economic circumstances
    c.   impatience, ambition, competitiveness, and a "hard-driving" approach to life
    d.   the tendency to explain bad events in negative, self-blaming ways

20.   Social support is an effective resource for coping with stress and involves

    a.   being cared for by the state until the person is able to cope on his or her own again
    b.   the presence of others that one can confide in and from whom one can expect help and concern
    c.   financial resources provided by social service agencies for people experiencing catastrophic stress
    d.   both a and c

ANSWERS

FILL-IN EXERCISES

1. peripheral   2. Cannon-Bard   3. women; men   4. display rules 5. basic   6. left; right   7. moods
8. Schachter-Singer; arousal   9. exposure 10. psychobiological; transactional   11. resistance
12. primary   13. stress   14. acculturative   15. catastrophes   16. antibodies   17. Type A   18. problem;
emotion

SAMPLE TEST QUESTIONS

1.	a	11.	c
2.	d	12.	d
3.	d	13.	c
4.	a	14.	d
5.	b	15.	b
6.	c	16.	b
7.	d	17.	b
8.	d	18.	a
9.	c	19.	a
10.	c	20.	b

Chapter 12
Personality

PART ONE: PRE-READ AND WORK
Outline and Learning Objectives

Pre-read this chapter's table of contents and end-of-chapter summary. Then, use the outline segment-by-segment to help you work through the chapter. Jot down your own questions, comments, and notes in the space provided. Make a note of difficult areas that you will need to review (include page numbers). Then, answer the questions in the learning objectives section that follows. Check off those you are confident that you can answer well. Re-read the material in the text for the questions about which you are less confident. Record the important points from your reading in the space below each question.

OUTLINE

Psychodynamic Theories

Freud's Models

Object Relations Theories

One Step Further: Assessing Unconscious Patterns

Contributions and Limitations of Psychodynamic Theories

Cognitive Social Theories

Encoding and Personal Relevance

Expectancies and Competences

Self-Regulation

Contributions and Limitations of Cognitive-Social Theories

Trait Theories

Eysenck's Theory

The Five Factor Model

From Brain to Behavior: The Genetics of Personality

Is Personality Consistent?

Humanistic Theories

Personality and Culture

Central Questions: What Are the Elements of Personality, and How Stable Are We?

LEARNING OBJECTIVES

Upon completion of Chapter 12, you should be able to answer the following questions.

1.   Identify and describe the three types of mental processes comprising Freud's topographical model.

2.   What role does conflict play in an individual's actions?

3.   What are the major characteristics of each of the following psychosexual stages?

   Oral stage

   Anal stage

   Phallic stage

   Latency stage

   Genital stage

4.   How is identification linked to the Oedipus complex?

5.   What are the differences between girls and boys in terms of the Oedipus complex?

6.   How do primary process and secondary process thinking differ?

7.   Compare the roles of the id, ego, and superego.

8.   Identify seven defense mechanisms and describe how each functions.

9. What is the focus of object relations theories and how do these approaches differ from Freudian theory?

10. What are the major methods used by psychodynamic psychologists to assess unconscious patterns?

11. What are the major contributions and limitations of psychodynamic theories?

12. How do cognitive social theories of personality differ from both behaviorist and psychodynamic views?

13. How do people's expectancies and competences influence the actions they carry out?

14. What role is played by self-regulation in the execution of behavior?

15. What is the difference, according to Eysenck's theory, between traits, and types?

16. Describe the three psychological types identified by Eysenck.

17. Which five superordinate personality traits make up the *Big Five* factors?

18. What do studies comparing MZ and DZ twins reared together and apart reveal about the heritability of various personality traits?

19. Explain Walter Mischel's argument that circumstances largely determine people's behavior. What are the arguments against this notion?

20.   Can it be said that personality traits are consistent over time?

21.   What are four limitations of trait theory approaches to personality?

22.   How can interpersonal experiences distort an individual's personality development, according to Carl Rogers's person-centered approach?

23.   What do existentialists mean when they say that people, unlike other animals and physical objects, have no fixed nature and must essentially create themselves?

24.   What are the major contributions and limitations of humanistic approaches to personality?

25.   What is death anxiety and how has it been investigated experimentally?

26.   How are personality and culture related in the following four approaches?

Marx's approach

Freud's approach

The culture pattern approach

Interactionist approaches

PART TWO: REVIEW AND LEARN
Key Terms, Fill-In Exercises, Application and Using What You Have Learned

Before doing the exercises below, review the information you learned in this chapter. Reread the work you did in part one of this study guide chapter, plus the interim summaries and end-of-chapter summary in your textbook. Review any problem areas. Once you feel comfortable with the material, do the following exercises without referring to your notes or textbook. If you have difficulty with a term or question, mark it and come back to it. When you have finished an exercise, go back to your notes and the textbook to find the answers to the questions that gave you difficulty. Finally, check your answers (key terms against the textbook and the rest against the answer key).

KEY TERMS

Upon completion of Chapter 12, you should be able to define the following terms.

Personality _____

_____

Structure of personality _____

_____

Individual differences _____

_____

Psychodynamics _____

_____

Topographic model _____

_____

Conscious _____

_____

Preconscious _____

_____

Unconscious _____

_____

Ambivalence _____

_____

Conflict _____

_____

Compromise formations _____

_____

Drive, or instinct model _____

_____

Libido _____

_____

Psychosexual stages _____

_____

Freud's developmental model _____

_____

Oral stage _____

_____

Fixations _____

_____

Anal stage _____

_____

Regression _____

_____

Phallic stage _____

_____

Identification _____

_____

Oedipus complex _____

_____

Castration complex _____

_____

Penis envy _____

_____

Genital stage _____

_____

Latency stage _____

_____

Genital stage _____

_____

Structural model _____

_____

Id _____

_____

Primary process thinking   _____

_____

Superego   _____

_____

Ego   _____

_____

Secondary process thinking   _____

_____

Defense mechanisms   _____

_____

Repression   _____

_____

Denial   _____

_____

Projection   _____

_____

Reaction formation   _____

_____

Sublimation   _____

_____

Rationalization   _____

_____

Passive aggression   _____

_____

Object relations theories_____

_____

Object relations _____

_____

Relational theories   _____

_____

Life history methods   _____

_____

Projective tests _____

_____

Rorschach inkblot test   _____

_____

Personal constructs   _____

_____

Personal value _____

_____

Life tasks   _____

_____

Behavior-outcome expectancy   _____

_____

Self-efficacy expectancy _____

_____

Competences _____

_____

Self-regulation _____

_____

Traits _____

_____

Extroversion _____

_____

Neuroticism _____

_____

Psychoticism _____

_____

Big five factors (or Five Factor Model) _____

_____

Situational variables _____

_____

Temperament _____

_____

Person-by-environment interactions _____

_____

Humanistic approaches _____

_____

Person-centered approach   _____

_____

Phenomenal experience _____

_____

Empathy   _____

_____

True self   _____

_____

False self   _____

_____

Conditions of worth   _____

_____

Ideal self   _____

_____

Actualizing tendency   _____

_____

Existentialism _____

_____

Bad faith   _____

_____

Existential dread   _____

_____

Culture pattern approach   _____

_____

Interactionist approaches   _____

_____

FILL-IN EXERCISES

Fill in the word or words that best fit in the spaces below.

1.   The _____ of personality refers to the way enduring patterns of thought, feeling, motivation, and behavior are organized.

2.   The ways people vary from one another in their characteristics are referred to as _____ differences.

3.   Freud divided mental processes into three types: _____, _____, and _____.

4.   The term _____ refers to conflicting feelings or motives that affect people's behavior.

5.   The solutions people develop to maximize fulfillment of conflicting motives are referred to as _____ formations.

6.   Freud used the term _____ to refer to the sex drive.

7.   The term _____ means reverting to conflicts or modes of managing emotion characteristic of an earlier stage of development.

8.   The process of _____ involves making another person part of yourself, trying to become more like the person by adopting his or her attitudes and values.

9.   The _____ _____ refers to Freud's hypothesis that little boys want an exclusive relationship with their mothers, and little girls want an exclusive relationship with their fathers.

10.   During the _____ stage, children repress their sexual impulses and continue to identify with their same-sex parents.

11. The structural model posits three sets of mental forces or structures: _____, _____, and _____.

12. Rational, logical, and goal-directed thinking, characteristic of the ego, is referred to as _____ _____ thinking.

13. _____ is an unconscious mechanism that keeps thoughts or memories, that would be too threatening to acknowledge, from awareness.

14. _____ _____ is a defense mechanism whereby a person turns unacceptable feelings or impulses into their opposites.

15. George Kelly coined the term personal _____ to refer to mental representations of the people, places, things, and events that are significant to a person.

16. The importance individuals attach to various outcomes or potential outcomes, according to the cognitive social approach, is referred to as _____ value.

17. According to the cognitive social approach, whether people carry out various actions depends on both expectancies and _____.

18. A commonly used method of measuring traits involves having people answer questions about themselves by filling out a _____.

19. Openness to experience, conscientiousness, extroversion, agreeableness, and neuroticism are referred to as the _____ _____ factors by trait theorists.

20. According to Walter Mischel, _____ variables -- the circumstances in which people find themselves -- largely determine their behavior.

21. Inhibition to the unfamiliar, a cluster of attributes in children that includes shyness and anxiety in the face of novelty, appears to be an aspect of _____, a basic personality disposition heavily influenced by genes.

22. According to Carl Rogers, individuals often wear a mask, which he refers to as a _____ self, which is the result of their natural desire to gain the _____ regard of other people.

23. Rogers proposed that the primary motivation in humans is an _____ tendency -- a desire to fulfill the full range of needs that humans experience.

24. The recognition that life has no absolute value or meaning and that ultimately we all face death is a problem referred to as existential _____.

25. _____ approaches hold that personality, culture, and economics are all interrelated – that is, causality is multidirectional.

APPLICATION

With reference to Freud's psychosexual stages, explain the behavior of each of the following individuals.

1.   Brenda is an extremely insecure woman. She seems to be always concerned with what other people are thinking of her. She has a real need for the approval of others and can't seem to make any decisions on her own. She clings to people, as if she's afraid to let go in case they'll leave her.

2.   Ted is really stingy. He just won't share with anybody. Not only that, he's so concerned that everything be done "just so." You might call him obsessive. Hardly anybody can work with him, because he always insists that everything be done his way.

3.   Mary is the most disorganized person you've ever seen. Her room is an absolute mess. She never completes her assignments, because she always loses them. She's always late for class; in fact, she even missed an exam last term because she overslept.

4.   Bill always has something in his mouth, often a cigarette. Lately, he's been trying to quit smoking by chewing bubble gum (he blows bubbles all the time and pops them, even in class). When he's not smoking or chewing gum, you'll probably find him sucking on a lollipop.

5.   Steve spends all his free time in the gym, working out. He has muscles where most people don't even know there are muscles! When he's not in the gym, he's trying to impress women. It's really important to him that women are attracted to him.

USING WHAT YOU HAVE LEARNED

Identify the individual or approach most closely associated with each of the following concepts.

1.   Big Five factors
2.   Regression
3.   Positive regard
4.   Types
5.   Self-efficacy expectancy
6.   False self
7.   Repertory grid technique
8.   Primary process thinking
9.   Personal constructs

10.   Empathy
11.   Self-regulation
12.   Extroversion
13.   Libido
14.   Ideal self
15.   Existential dread
16.   Preconscious
17.   Personal value
18.   Competences

PART THREE: TEST AND KNOW
SAMPLE TEST QUESTIONS

Test how well you have learned this chapter's material by answering the sample test questions. You may wish to mark your answers on a separate sheet of paper so you can reuse this test for exam review. Once you have completed the exam, check your answers and then go back to your notes and the textbook to review questions you found difficult.

1.   Freud proposed two basic drives motivating human behavior:

   a.   sex and aggression   b.   aggression and violence
   c.   sex and survival   d.   aggression and destructiveness

2.   According to Freud, preconscious mental processes are

   a.   rational, goal-directed thoughts at the center of awareness
   b.   thoughts that are not conscious, but could become conscious at any time
   c.   irrational, inaccessible thoughts
   d.   inert, unconscious thoughts

3.   Which of Freud's stages is characterized by conflicts with parents about compliance and defiance?

   a.   oral   b.   anal
   c.   phallic   d.   latency

4.   The reservoir of sexual and aggressive energy is the

   a.   libido   b.   ego
   c.   id   d.   latency

5.   Fixations at the latency stage can lead to

   a.   conflicts about giving and receiving   b.   a preoccupation with attracting mates
   c.   exaggerated needs for approval   d.   asexuality

6.   Fixations at the oral stage can lead to

   a.   conflicts about giving and receiving   b.   a preoccupation with attracting mates
   c.   exaggerated needs for approval   d.   asexuality

7.   Secondary process thinking is characteristic of the

   a.   libido   b.   ego
   c.   id   d.   anima

8. Converting sexual or aggressive impulses into socially acceptable activities involves the defense mechanism of

    a. denial   b. projection
    c. rationalization   d. sublimation

9. A hard-driving businessman, who thinks his competitors, suppliers, and customers are always trying to cheat him, may in fact be the one with questionable ethics. To recognize his own greed and lack of concern for others would conflict with his conscience. So, instead, he sees these traits in others. This defense mechanism is known as

    a. denial   b. reaction formation
    c. rationalization   d. projection

10. A student who plagiarizes her term paper and justifies her actions by saying that passing the course will help her earn her public policy degree and serve the community, is using the defense mechanism of _____ to justify her dishonesty.

    a. rationalization   b. sublimation
    c. denial   d. passive aggression

11. Object relations theories explain difficulties people have in maintaining intimate relationships in terms of

    a. unconscious conflicts
    b. a natural desire to gain the positive regard of other people
    c. maladaptive interpersonal patterns laid down in the first few years of life
    d. the recognition that life has no absolute value or meaning and that ultimately we will all face death

12. George Kelly and his colleagues developed the _____ to assess individuals' personal constructs indirectly.

    a. repertory grid technique   b. Thematic Apperception Test (TAT)
    c. Rorschach inkblot test   d. person-centered approach

13. Self-regulation refers to

    a. setting goals   b. evaluating one's performance
    c. adjusting one's behavior to meet goals d. all of the above

14. Extroversion, neuroticism, and psychoticism are three psychological types identified by

    a. Kelly   b. Rogers
    c. Eysenck   d. Adler

15.   Which of the following is *not* used to measure traits?

    a.   asking people to report on the content of their dreams
    b.   observing people's behavior over time and in different situations
    c.   asking people who know the individual well to fill out questionnaires about his or her personality
    d.   asking people themselves to fill out a self-report questionnaire

16.   The Big Five factors include

    a.   extroversion, agreeableness, conscientiousness, neuroticism, and openness to experience
    b.   extroversion, neuroticism, psychoticism, conscientiousness, and openness to experience
    c.   extroversion, expectancies, competences, self-efficacy, and openness to experience
    d.   extroversion, personal values, conscientiousness, neuroticism, and ill-temperedness

17.   Which of the following is a criticism of trait theory approaches?

    a.   They overemphasize the rational side of life and underemphasize the emotional, motivational, and irrational.
    b.   They are no more sophisticated than the theories of personality held by lay people.
    c.   They have failed to develop a substantial body of testable hypotheses and research.
    d.   They are theories aimed at interpretation of behavior that has already occurred, rather than at prediction of behavior.

18.   In Carl Rogers's view, psychology should try to understand

    a.   how beliefs, rituals, and institutions shape individuals
    b.   the ways in which unconscious conflicts underlie an individual's behavior
    c.   the way people conceive of reality and experience themselves and their world
    d.   that life has no absolute value or meaning and that ultimately we all face death

19.   According to Rogers, the fundamental tool of the psychologist is

    a.   the repertory grid technique
    b.   empathy
    c.   projective tests like the TAT and Rorschach inkblot test
    d.   direct observation of an individual across many situations

20.   The notion that people's needs, wishes, beliefs, and values are products of the conditions under which they live and work was proposed by

    a.   Karl Marx   b.   Jean-Jacques Rousseau
    c.   Jean-Paul Sartre   d.   George Kelly

ANSWERS

FILL-IN EXERCISES

1. structure   2. individual   3. conscious, preconscious, unconscious   4. ambivalence 5. compromise
6. libido 7. regression   8. identification   9. Oedipus complex 10. latency   11. id, ego, superego
12. secondary process   13. repression   14. reaction formation   15. constructs   16. personal
17. competences 18. questionnaire 19. Big Five   20. situational   21. temperament   22. false; positive
23. actualizing   24. dread   25. interactionist

APPLICATION

1. oral stage fixation
2. anal stage fixation
3. anal stage fixation
4. oral stage fixation
5. phallic stage fixation

USING WHAT YOU HAVE LEARNED

1.	trait		10.	humanistic (Rogers)
2.	psychodynamic (Freud)		11.	cognitive social
3.	humanistic (Rogers)		12.	trait (Eysenck)
4.	trait (Eysenck)		13.	psychodynamic (Freud)
5.	cognitive social (Bandura)		14.	humanistic (Rogers)
6.	humanistic (Rogers)		15.	existential
7.	cognitive social (Kelly)		16.	psychodynamic (Freud)
8.	psychodynamic (Freud)		17.	cognitive social
9.	cognitive social (Kelly)		18.	cognitive social

SAMPLE TEST QUESTIONS

1.	a		11.	c
2.	b		12.	a
3.	b		13.	d
4.	c		14.	c
5.	d		15.	a
6.	c		16.	a
7.	b		17.	b
8.	d		18.	c
9.	d		19.	b
10.	a		20.	a

Chapter 13
Physical and
Cognitive Development

PART ONE: PRE-READ AND WORK
Outline and Learning Objectives

Pre-read this chapter's table of contents and end-of-chapter summary. Then, use the outline segment-by-segment to help you work through the chapter. Jot down your own questions, comments, and notes in the space provided. Make a note of difficult areas that you will need to review (include page numbers). Then, answer the questions in the learning objectives section that follows. Check off those you are confident that you can answer well. Re-read the material in the text for the questions about which you are less confident. Record the important points from your reading in the space below each question.

OUTLINE

Central Questions in Developmental Psychology

Nature and Nurture

The Relative Importance of Early Experience

Stages or Continuous Change?

Studying Development

Cross-Sectional Studies

Longitudinal Studies

Sequential Studies

Physical Development and Its Psychological Consequences

Prenatal Development

From Brain to Behavior: The Development of the Nervous System

Infancy

Childhood and Adolescence

Adulthood and Aging

A Global Vista: Menopause in a Mayan Village

Cognitive Development in Infancy, Childhood, and Adolescence

Perceptual and Cognitive Development in Infancy

Piaget's Theory of Cognitive Development

The Information-Processing Approach to Cognitive Development

Integrative Theories of Cognitive Development

Cognitive Development and Change in Adulthood

Cognitive Changes Associated with Aging

Aging and "Senility"

Central Questions: The Nature of Development

LEARNING OBJECTIVES

Upon completion of Chapter 13, you should be able to answer the following questions.

1. What is meant by the term critical period? Why is this concept controversial when considering human development?

2. How does continuous developmental change differ from change that is stage-like?

3. What are the advantages and disadvantages of three types of research design used by developmental psychologists?

4. What are the three periods of prenatal development?

5. What is meant by the term *teratogen*? Describe the prenatal effects of the following three teratogens: alcohol, crack cocaine, and maternal stress.

6. Describe how the nervous system develops after birth.

7. What are the characteristics of puberty and what differences are there between boys and girls in the effects of early maturation?

8. What are the major consequences of menopause and how can culture influence women's reactions to this event?

9. What are the changes in male sexuality that begin at mid-life?

10.   What is "ageism"?

11.   What methods do researchers use to study infant perception and cognition?

12.   Describe the visual and auditory capabilities of infants.

13.   What has been found concerning intermodal understanding in infants?

14.   What has research shown concerning memory in infants?

15.   How are assimilation and accommodation involved in the process of adaptation to the environment?

16.   What are the major characteristics and the approximate age-range of each of Piaget's four stages of cognitive development?

17.   What is "object permanence," and approximately when does this concept develop?

18.   How is "centration" related to the concept of "conservation?"

19.   Explain the major criticisms of Piaget's theory.

20.   How does the information-processing approach to cognitive development differ from Piaget's approach?

21.   Describe the following five important factors that information-processing theorists believe influence children's cognitive efficiency – processing speed, knowledge base, automatic processing, cognitive strategies, and metacognition.

22.   How does Case's model integrate Piagetian and information-processing views of cognitive development?

23.   What is "psychomotor slowing?" How can this affect cognitive performance in the elderly?

24.   How does memory change in the elderly? What aspects of memory decline with age? What aspects are relatively unaffected by age?

25.   In what ways do fluid intelligence and crystallized intelligence change with increasing age?

26.   What are the characteristics and possible causes of Alzheimer's disease?

PART TWO: REVIEW AND LEARN
Key Terms, Fill-In Exercises, Application and Using What You Have Learned

Before doing the exercises below, review the information you learned in this chapter. Reread the work you did in part one of this study guide chapter, plus the interim summaries and end-of-chapter summary in your textbook. Review any problem areas. Once you feel comfortable with the material, do the following exercises without referring to your notes or textbook. If you have difficulty with a term or question, mark it and come back to it. When you have finished an exercise, go back to your notes and the textbook to find the answers to the questions that gave you difficulty. Finally, check your answers (key terms against the textbook and the rest against the answer key).

KEY TERMS

Upon completion of Chapter 13, you should be able to define the following terms.

Developmental psychology _____

_____

Maturation _____

_____

Critical periods _____

_____

Sensitive periods _____

_____

Stages _____

_____

Cross-sectional studies _____

_____

Cohort effects _____

_____

Longitudinal studies_____

_____

Sequential studies _____

_____

Teratogens _____

_____

Plasticity _____

_____

Puberty _____

_____

Presbycusis _____

_____

Ageism _____

_____

Intermodal processing _____

_____

Infantile amnesia _____

_____

Assimilation _____

_____

Schema _____

_____

Accommodation _____

_____

Equilibration _____

_____

Structure of thought _____

_____

Operations _____

_____

Sensorimotor stage _____

_____

Object permanence _____

_____

Egocentric _____

_____

Preoperational stage _____

_____

Operations _____

_____

Concrete operational stage _____

_____

Conservation _____

_____

Formal operational stage _____

_____

Knowledge base _____

_____

Automatization _____

_____

Metacognition _____

_____

Neo-Piagetian theorists _____

_____

Psychomotor slowing _____

_____

Dementia _____

_____

Alzheimer's disease _____

_____

FILL-IN EXERCISES

Fill in the word or words that best fit in the spaces below.

1.   Studies of children who have experienced extreme deprivation during their early years provide evidence for _____ periods in humans, times that are important to subsequent development, although perhaps not absolutely critical for future psychological growth.

2.   Some psychologists view development as occurring in stages, where behavior at one stage is not just quantitatively different from behavior at another stage, but _____ different.

3.   Cross-sectional studies are most useful when _____ effects (i.e., differences among age groups associated with differences in culture) are minimal.

4.   A _____ design combines cross-sectional and _____ comparisons, solving most of the problems of both of these types of design.

5.   The _____ period begins at about the ninth week of prenatal development.

6.   The first two weeks after conception are referred to as the _____ period.

7. _____ are environmental agents that can harm a developing fetus or embryo.

8. When touched on its cheek, an infant turns its head and opens its mouth to suck. This pattern of behavior is referred to as the _____ _____.

9. In general, the development of motor skills in infants progress from _____ to _____.

10. *Early* onset of puberty tends to be associated with _____ *(more/less)* distress for boys than for girls.

11. For women the most dramatic physical change of middle adulthood is _____.

12. The visual acuity of the newborn is estimated to be approximately _____, but improves to approximately _____ by six months.

13. Most people completely lack explicit memory for events before age 3 or 4, a phenomenon known as _____ _____.

14. Interpreting actions or events in terms of one's present schemas is referred to as _____, whereas _____ refers to the modification of schemas to fit reality.

15. The _____ stage lasts from birth until about 2 years of age.

16. The preoperational stage is characterized by the emergence of _____ thought.

17. _____ refers to the preoperational child's tendency to focus on one perceptually striking feature of an object without considering other features that might be relevant.

18. In the _____ operational stage children are capable of mentally manipulating abstract as well as concrete objects, events, and ideas.

19. In contrast to Piaget's theory which focuses on changes occurring in stages, the information-processing perspective focuses on changes that are _____.

20. Compared to adults, children's _____ _____ (their accumulated knowledge) are limited because of their relative inexperience with life.

21. _____ refers to the process of thinking about thinking.

22. Theorists who attempt to integrate Piaget's theory with information-processing views are sometimes referred to as _____-Piagetian theorists.

23. _____ _____ is a progressive and incurable illness, that occurs later in life, and causes severe impairment of memory, reasoning, language, and behavior.

APPLICATION

Situation

Mickey and his older brother Dave are having lunch. When their mother gives them their juice, Mickey's glass is short and fat, while Dave's is tall and thin. Although their mother is careful to pour the same amount of juice into each glass, Mickey complains that Dave got more. Their mother gets a short, fat glass from the cupboard and, while Mickey watches, pours Dave's juice from the tall, thin glass into the new short, fat one. Mickey says "That's better, now they're the same." After watching his mother pour the juice from one glass into the other, Dave just sits there chuckling. He whispers to his mother, "Boy, did you ever fool Mickey! It's the same amount of juice in both glasses!"

Questions to answer

1.   Which of Piaget's stages of cognitive development most likely describes Mickey? How about Dave?

2.   What does Dave realize that Mickey doesn't? What is this concept called?

3.   According to Piaget's theory, what is it that causes Mickey to think there is more juice in the second glass? What is this process called?

USING WHAT YOU HAVE LEARNED

The chapter discusses the phenomenon of *ageism*, a prejudice against old people. It describes how subjects in a priming experiment more readily associated negative traits with the word "old" and positive traits with the word "young." These findings could reflect the stereotypes people apply to the elderly. Stereotypical beliefs about old people are actually relatively common. To get an idea of these beliefs, ask several of your friends what "old" people are like and how they differ from young people.

1.   What seem to be the most common stereotypical beliefs?

2.   Is there an age difference in beliefs? Do older people have the same beliefs as younger people? If they do, could these actually be a self-fulfilling prophecy?

3.   Are any of these beliefs based on fact? Compare people's beliefs with what you have read about aging in this chapter. How accurate are people's beliefs?

4.   Does providing objective information about aging alter people's beliefs. A good way to answer this would be to consider your own beliefs *before* and *after* reading Chapter 13. Did they change?

PART THREE: TEST AND KNOW
SAMPLE TEST QUESTIONS

Test how well you have learned this chapter's material by answering the sample test questions. You may wish to mark your answers on a separate sheet of paper so you can reuse this test for exam review. Once you have completed the exam, check your answers and then go back to your notes and the textbook to review questions you found difficult.

1. When considering the roles of nature and nurture, the question(s) asked by developmental psychologists is (are)

   a. *Which* is more important in development-- nature or nurture?
   b. *How much* does each contribute to development?
   c. *How* do nature and nurture contribute interactively to development?
   d. all of the above

2. Relatively discrete steps in development, through which everyone passes in the same sequence, are referred to as

   a. sensitive periods   b. critical periods
   c. cohorts   d. stages

3. A research design used by developmental psychologists, which follows multiple cohorts longitudinally, is referred to as a

   a. sequential study   b. cross-sectional study
   c. longitudinal study   d. cohort study

4. By about _____ weeks, the fetus is capable of sustaining life on its own.

   a. 16   b. 22
   c. 28   d. 32

5. Physical deformities, as well as learning disabilities, behavior problems, and attention difficulties are associated with prenatal exposure to

   a. alcohol   b. iron
   c. crack cocaine   d. nicotine

6. Which of the following does NOT decrease in older adults?

   a. crystallized intelligence b. ability to hear high-frequencies
   c. sexual desire   d. visual sensitivity to contrasts

7.   Which of the following responses have been used to assess infant perception?

    a.   rooting reflex and sucking   b.   orienting reflex and fixation time
    c.   equilibration and disequilibration   d.   assimilation and accommodation

8.   For Piaget, the driving force behind cognitive development is

    a.   assimilation   b.   accommodation
    c.   equilibration   d.   schemas

9.   Piaget referred to the process of modifying schemas to fit reality as

    a.   adaptation   b.   accommodation
    c.   assimilation   d.   equilibration

10.   A major achievement of the sensorimotor stage is the development of

    a.   decentration   b.   conservation
    c.   operations   d.   object permanence

11.   Little Stacey loves playing peek-a-boo. Her favorite part is to cover her eyes with her hands and then call out "Nobody can see me!". Stacey is likely in which of Piaget's stages of cognitive development?

    a.   formal operational   b.   preoperational
    c.   sensorimotor   d.   concrete operational

12.   "If Louise is older than Carol, and Carol is older than Christine, which girl is the youngest?" This type of question requires an understanding of

    a.   centration   b.   conservation
    c.   egocentrism   d.   transitivity

13.   During which stage are children first able to readily solve problems like the one above?

    a.   formal operational   b.   sensorimotor
    c.   preoperational   d.   concrete operational

14.   Which of the following is NOT a criticism of Piaget's theory?

    a.   He focused too heavily on the kind of rational thinking typical of scientific or philosophical pursuits.
    b.   He assumed that a child's thinking tends to "be" at one stage or another.
    c.   He overestimated the capacities of infants and preschool children.
    d.   He failed to pay enough attention to the role of culture in development.

15.   Children's understanding of the way they perform cognitive tasks, such as remembering, learning, and solving problems, is referred to as

    a.   metacognition
    b.   cognitive strategies
    c.   knowledge base
    d.   automatic processing

16.   According to Case, the most important factor in qualitative changes in cognitive development (that is, movement across stages) is an increasing

    a.   capacity for abstract thinking
    b.   ability to make use of metamemory
    c.   capacity for working memory
    d.   ability to perform operations

17.   The problems older people have with long-term memory appear largely to be in the

    a.   encoding of implicit memories
    b.   retrieval of explicit memories
    c.   storage of information
    d.   area of recognition memory

18.   One of the clearest changes that accompanies aging is

    a.   a decline in crystallized intelligence
    b.   a decline in abstract reasoning abilities
    c.   an erosion of the knowledge base
    d.   psychomotor slowing

19.   Fluid intelligence

    a.   peaks in young adulthood, then levels off, and begins declining by mid adulthood
    b.   increases throughout most of life, showing declines only in very old age
    c.   begins declining shortly after the preschool period, although the decline is imperceptibly slow at first
    d.   peaks at puberty, then begins a decline that accelerates with age

20.   Alzheimer's patients have abnormally low levels of _____, a neurotransmitter that plays a central role in memory functioning.

    a.   acetylcholine
    b.   serotonin
    c.   norepinephrine
    d.   GABA

ANSWERS

FILL-IN EXERCISES

1. sensitive 2. qualitatively 3. cohort 4. sequential; longitudinal 5. fetal 6. germinal 7. teratogens
8. rooting reflex 9. head, toe 10. less 11. menopause 12. 20/500; 20/100 13. infantile amnesia
14. assimilation; accommodation 15. sensorimotor 16. symbolic 17. centration 18. formal
19. continuous (or quantitative) 20. knowledge bases 21. metacognition 22. neo
23. Alzheimer's disease

APPLICATION

1.   Mickey is preoperational. Dave is concrete or formal operational.

2.   Dave realizes that the amount of juice in the glass has remained the same, even though the size and shape of the glass have changed. In other words, the basic properties of an object remain stable even though its superficial properties may be changed. This is referred to as *conservation*

3.   Mickey focuses only on one aspect of the glass -- its height, and ignores the difference between the two glasses in width. *Centration*

SAMPLE TEST QUESTIONS

1.	c	11.	b
2.	d	12.	d
3.	a	13.	d
4.	c	14.	c
5.	a	15.	a
6.	a	16.	c
7.	b	17.	b
8.	c	18.	d
9.	b	19.	a
10.	d	20.	a

Chapter 14
Social Development

PART ONE: PRE-READ AND WORK
Outline and Learning Objectives

Pre-read this chapter's table of contents and end-of-chapter summary. Then, use the outline segment-by-segment to help you work through the chapter. Jot down your own questions, comments, and notes in the space provided. Make a note of key terms and of difficult areas that you will need to review (include page numbers). Then, answer the questions in the learning objectives section that follows. Check off those you are confident that you can answer well. Re-read the material in the text for the questions about which you are less confident. Record the important points from your reading in the space below each question.

OUTLINE

Attachment

Attachment in Infancy

Individual Differences in Attachment Patterns

From Brain to Behavior: Temperament, Experience, and their Interaction in the Development of Attachment Styles

Implications of Attachment for Later Development

Socialization

The Role of Parents

The Role of Culture

A Global Vista: Parental Acceptance and Rejection in Cross-Cultural Perspective

Socialization of Gender

Peer Relationships

Friendships

Sibling Relationships

Development of Social Cognition

The Evolving Self-Concept

Concepts of Others

Perspective-Taking and Theory of Mind

Children's Understanding of Gender

Moral Development

The Role of Cognition

The Role of Emotion

Commentary: Making Sense of Moral Development

Social Development Across the Lifespan

Erikson's Theory of Psychosocial Development

Development from Adolescence through Old Age

Central Questions: Nature and Nurture, Cognition, and Emotion

LEARNING OBJECTIVES

Upon completion of Chapter 14, you should be able to answer the following questions.

1.   What is imprinting and how is it similar to attachment?

2.   How do the Strange Situation behaviors of infants with secure, avoidant, ambivalent, and disorganized attachment styles differ?

3.   What are internal working models of relationships?

4.   How may temperament and experience influence attachment?

5.   How does the later adjustment of securely attached infants differ from that of insecurely attached infants?

6.   What is meant by adult attachment style? How is the attachment style of parents related to that of their infants?

7.   Can individuals overcome the effects of early negative attachment experiences?

8.   What are the characteristics and effects of each of the three styles of parenting identified by Diana Baumrind?

9.   Discuss how parental acceptance and rejection may differ across cultures, yet be similar in their effects.

10.   What role do adults play in the socialization of gender roles?

11.   What changes take place across age in the meaning of friendship to children and in the roles that friends play?

12.   How do "rejected" children differ from "neglected" children?

13.   What are the characteristics of sibling relationships?

14.   How do children's descriptions of themselves and others change across age?.

15.   How is the development of "theory of mind" related to perspective taking?

16.   What changes occur across age in children's perspective taking?

17.   Compare between the following three stages of children's understanding of gender: gender identity, gender stability, gender constancy.

18.   What are gender schemas?

19.   Discuss the biological/evolutionary and cultural/social-learning explanations for gender differences in aggression and nurturance.

20.   How do Piaget's stages of morality of constraint and morality of cooperation differ?

21.   What are Kohlberg's three levels of moral reasoning? Provide examples of answers to the Heinz dilemma for each level.

22.   According to the social-cognitive view, how is prosocial behavior acquired?

23.   Outline the sequence of judgments that comprise the information-processing model of moral decision making.

24.   Explain the psychodynamic view of moral development.

25.   How does empathy develop in children?

26.   What are the advantages and shortcomings associated with the cognitive and emotional approaches to moral development?

27.   What is the major crisis or developmental task of each of Erikson's eight stages of psychosocial development?

28.   How do the conflict and continuity models differ in their view of adolescence?

29.   What factors have been found to have the potential to interfere with marital intimacy and satisfaction with marriage?

30.   Is there really a "midlife crisis?"

31.   What factors have been found to predict happiness and satisfaction in old age?

PART TWO: REVIEW AND LEARN
Key Terms, Fill-In Exercises, Application and Using What You Have Learned

Before doing the exercises below, review the information you learned in this chapter. Reread the work you did in part one of this study guide chapter, plus the interim summaries and end-of-chapter summary in your textbook. Review any problem areas. Once you feel comfortable with the material, do the following exercises without referring to your notes or textbook. If you have difficulty with a term or question, mark it and come back to it. When you have finished an exercise, go back to your notes and the textbook to find the answers to the questions that gave you difficulty. Finally, check your answers (key terms against the textbook and the rest against the answer key).

KEY TERMS

Social development   _____

_____

Attachment   _____

_____

Imprinting   _____

_____

Separation anxiety   _____

_____

Secure attachment style   _____

_____

Avoidant attachment style   _____

_____

Ambivalent attachment style   _____

_____

Disorganized attachment style   _____

_____

Internal working models   _____

_____

Adult attachment   _____

_____

Socialization   _____

_____

Authoritarian parents   _____

_____

Permissive parents   _____

_____

Authoritative parents   _____

_____

Gender roles   _____

_____

Gender _____

_____

Sex typing   _____

_____

Rejected children _____

_____

Neglected children _____

_____

Social cognition _____

_____

Self-concept _____

_____

Perspective-taking _____

_____

Theory of mind _____

_____

Gender identity _____

_____

Gender stability _____

_____

Gender constancy _____

_____

Gender schemas _____

_____

Sex-role ideology _____

_____

Morality of constraint   _____

_____

Morality of cooperation   _____

_____

Preconventional morality   _____

_____

Conventional morality   _____

_____

Postconventional morality   _____

_____

Prosocial behavior   _____

_____

Empathy   _____

_____

Empathic distress   _____

_____

Psychosocial stages   _____

_____

Developmental task   _____

_____

Basic trust versus mistrust   _____

_____

Autonomy versus shame and doubt _____

_____

Initiative versus guilt _____

_____

Industry versus inferiority _____

_____

Identity versus identity confusion_____

_____

Identity _____

_____

Identity confusion _____

_____

Initiation rites _____

_____

Negative identity _____

_____

Intimacy versus isolation _____

_____

Generativity versus stagnation _____

_____

Generativity _____

_____

Stagnation   _____

_____

Integrity versus despair _____

_____

Conflict model _____

_____

Continuity model   _____

_____

FILL-IN EXERCISES

Fill in the word or words that best fit in the spaces below.

1.   The term _____ refers to the tendency of young animals of certain species to follow an animal to which they were exposed during a sensitive period early in their lives.

2.   The attachment figure serves as a safe _____ from which children can explore the environment, and to whom they can periodically return for "emotional refueling."

3.   Babies visually recognize their mother at about _____ months of age and, by about _____ or _____ months, recognize and greet their mothers and other attachment figures from across the room.

4.   Cross-cultural research, as well as research with blind infants, suggest a _____ basis for separation anxiety.

5.   In the Strange Situation, infants who welcome their mother after her absence and seek closeness with her have a _____ attachment style.

6.   Bowlby proposed that infants develop _____ _____ models, or mental representations of attachment relationships, which form the basis for expectations in close relationships.

7.   Adults with an attachment style characterized as _____ (similar to the disorganized style seen in infancy) have difficulty speaking coherently about attachment figures from their past and have generally been unable to cope with losses or other traumatic experiences from their past.

8.   _____ involves learning the rules, beliefs, values, skills, attitudes, and behavior patterns of society.

9. Parents who place a high value on obedience and respect for authority are described as _____ parents; those who impose virtually no controls on their children are referred to as _____ parents; while those who set and enforce standards, but also encourage give and take are called _____ parents.

10. While the term sex refers to a biological classification based on genetic and anatomical differences, the term _____ refers to the psychological meaning of being male or female, which is influenced by _____.

11. Friendships marked by commitment and reciprocity (sharing and give and take) first begin to emerge around age _____.

12. Adolescents are more concerned than younger children with _____ in friendships.

13. Children who are rarely picked by their classmates as either someone they really like or someone they really dislike are referred to as _____ children.

14. Children's understanding of themselves, others, and relationships is referred to as _____ _____.

15. The term _____ _____ refers to an organized view of ourselves or way of representing information about the self.

16. _____ _____ refers to the ability to understand other people's viewpoints.

17. The ability to categorize oneself as either male or female is called _____ _____ and usually is attained by about _____ years of age.

18. Gender _____ occurs when children learn that a person's gender cannot be altered by changes in appearance or activities.

19. The term _____ refers to the set of rules people use to balance the conflicting interests of themselves and others.

20. Viewing social rules as unchanging and unchangeable is one of the characteristics of the stage Piaget called the morality of _____.

21. According to Kohlberg's theory, the desire to gain the approval or avoid the disapproval of others is one characteristic of the level of _____ morality.

22. According to the _____ model, moral reasoning involves making a series of sequential judgments about whether an act is immoral and whether it deserves punishment.

23. The psychodynamic view of moral development proposes that children start out relatively _____, or self-centered and interested in gratifying their own needs.

24.   Discrepancies between what people feel they should do and what they contemplate or observe themselves doing result in _____.

25.   As children become better able to distinguish their own thoughts and feelings from those of others, they begin to experience genuine _____ distress – feeling upset for another person – which motivates moral or prosocial behavior.

26.   Erikson's model is comprised of eight _____ stages of development.

27.   The third of Erikson's stages is called "*initiative versus* _____." The next stage is "_____ *versus inferiority*."

28.   Some adolescents adopt a _____ _____, taking on a role that society defines as bad, but which provides them with a sense that at least they are something.

29.   To Erikson, the opposite of "*generativity*" is _____.

30.   Erikson's final stage is "_____ *versus* _____."

USING WHAT YOU HAVE LEARNED

A group of students has just covered social development in their Introduction to Psychology course. The topic of attachment in infancy was particularly interesting, and a topic they hadn't given much thought to, previously. The students get into a discussion concerning whether attachment is important and what role a mother plays in her infant's attachment. Your job is to decide whether each student's opinion is accurate or not, based on your readings in the text.

Student #1: "As far as I'm concerned, attachment isn't very important. Sure you can't just ignore babies; you have to feed them and change them. But all this 'lovey-dovey' stuff just makes their parents feel good. It's not important for the baby. How babies feel about their mothers isn't important in the long run."

Student #2: "Well, I think attachment is VERY important! Once a baby has formed an insecure attachment, there isn't very much you can do to change things. They'll be messed up for life!"

Student #3: "I've been thinking about what causes insecure attachment and it's got to be the mother's fault. Mothers are totally to blame if their baby is insecurely attached. It has to do with how they treat their baby, and that's all there is to it."

Student #4: "I think there's too much 'mother-bashing' that goes on when people talk about attachment. Everybody says it's the mother's fault. So if a baby isn't securely attached, who gets blamed? The mother! What a load of guilt to put on someone. What about the baby? Are babies all the same? Aren't some babies more easily scared than others, no matter what their mother does?"

APPLICATION

In Chapter 14, you learned about the challenges or developmental tasks faced by individuals at different stages in their lives, according to Erikson's theory. Each of the descriptions that follow translates one of Erikson's developmental tasks into a conflict faced by a particular individual. For each description, match the psychosocial stage that corresponds to the challenge they're facing. (Note: Some stages appear more than once.)

Psychosocial Stages

Basic Trust versus Mistrust

Autonomy versus Shame and Doubt

Initiative versus Guilt

Industry versus Inferiority

Identity versus Identity Confusion

Intimacy versus Isolation

Generativity versus Stagnation

Integrity versus Despair

Conflicts

1. Paul is a "professional student." He has studied engineering, general arts, history, psychology, and criminology. Now, he feels maybe he should leave university and try business for a while.

2. Monica spends a lot of time playing make-believe. She enjoys dressing up in adult clothes, pretending to be the role she dresses as. She loves dreaming up ideas and carrying them out.

3. Ronny loves sports at school. He's quite athletic and is always trying to show that he's better than anyone else on the soccer team.

4. Since her kids left home, Diane has been toying with the idea of becoming a scout leader. She thought she'd like all the time she'd have to herself when the kids grew up, but, in fact, she finds her life feels really empty with them gone.

5. Sarah hangs out with a group of skin heads. They hang around the shopping plaza doing nothing and seem to delight in offending some of the shoppers by their foul language and appearance.

6. Ian has been avoiding Jennifer. He likes her and she likes him. But, he's afraid to get too close. Their relationship is starting to get serious and that scares Ian.

7. Geoff has been having problems with reading at school. Compared to other kids he's far behind. It's especially hard when they take turns reading aloud. He slouches down in his desk and tries to hide so that the teacher won't call on him.

8. Guy has run a successful TV repair business for 20 years. Last year he sold the business to spend his time teaching TV repair to physically disabled teenagers.

9. Sonia is always trying to do things on her own. She seems proud of the fact that she can now stand on her own two feet. In fact, she often insists on doing things like feeding herself, even if it means getting the food all over herself.

PART THREE: TEST AND KNOW
SAMPLE TEST QUESTIONS

Test how well you have learned this chapter's material by answering the sample test questions. You may wish to mark your answers on a separate sheet of paper so you can reuse this test for exam review. Once you have completed the exam, check your answers and then go back to your notes and the textbook to review questions you found difficult.

1.   Separation anxiety emerges at about the same time as

    a.   the infant is able to stand alone
    b.   the infant begins to walk
    c.   the infant is weaned
    d.   the infant begins to crawl

2.   Sally was very upset when her mother left her alone in the Strange Situation. When her mother returned, Sally was angry and rejecting, yet at the same time sought to be close to her. Sally's attachment pattern is best described as

    a.   disorganized
    b.   securely attached
    c.   ambivalent
    d.   avoidant

3.   The temperamental variable that is most highly predictive of attachment status across several studies is:

    a.   slowness to warm up
    b.   susceptibility to stress
    c.   negative affect
    d.   empathic distress

4.   Adults who dismiss the importance of attachment relationships or offer idealized generalizations about their parents, but are unable to back them up with specific examples, tend to display a(n) _____ adult attachment style.

    a.   secure   b.   ambivalent
    c.   avoidant   d.   unresolved

5.   Parents who place high value on obedience and respect for authority and do not encourage discussion of *why* particular behaviors are important are described as

    a.   authoritarian   b.   permissive
    c.   authoritative   d.   disorganized

6.   Low self-reliance and poor impulse control is associated with which parenting style?

    a.   authoritarian   b.   permissive
    c.   authoritative   d.   disorganized

7.   Parents often treat their sons and daughters differently from an early age. Girls in Europe and North America, in contrast to boys receive more

    a.   punishment.
    b.   encouragement to compete.
    c.   warmth, affection, and trust.
    d.   pressure not to cry.

8.   Neglected children tend to be

    a.   ignored by their peers
    b.   disliked by their peers
    c.   hostile and aggressive
    d.   at risk for later delinquency

9.   When asked to describe himself, Sid replies "I'm good at math, and I'm the best skateboarder in my school." Based on his description, Sid is likely around

    a.   3 years of age
    b.   6 years of age
    c.   9 years of age
    d.   17 years of age

10.   In the game "Decoy and Defender" a child simply moves her flag carrier as quickly as possible across the board, totally failing to take into account her opponent's perspective. Such an egocentric strategy would be typical of a(n)

    a.   1- to 2-year-old child
    b.   3- to 6-year-old child
    c.   6- to 8-year-old child
    d.   8- to 10-year-old child

11.   Gender constancy refers to children's

    a.   tendency to play and form friendships primarily with same-sex peers
    b.   realization that their gender remains constant over time
    c.   ability to categorize themselves and others according to gender
    d.   realization that a person's gender cannot be altered by changes in appearance or activities

12.   Mental representations that associate psychological characteristics with each sex are referred to as

    a.   gender schemas   b.   gender roles
    c.   sex typing   d.   gender constancy

13.   The majority of preindustrial societies socialize boys from an early age to be

    a.   self-reliant   b.   self-restrained
    c.   responsible   d.   obedient

14.   When one child tries to change the rules to a game of marbles, the child she is playing with gets very upset, shouting "You're not allowed to break the rules!" The second child is likely at which level of moral development?

    a.   morality of cooperation
    b.   postconventional morality
    c.   morality of constraint
    d.   conventional morality

15.   After listening to the dilemma of Heinz and the druggist, an individual responds that Heinz should steal the drug, because the value of human life is far more important than obeying the law. This answer is characteristic of which of Kohlberg's levels of moral development?

    a.   morality of cooperation
    b.   postconventional morality
    c.   morality of constraint
    d.   conventional morality

16.   According to cognitive-social theories of moral development, children learn that certain acts are wrong and will be punished because they

    a.   are punished for the act
    b.   see someone else punished
    c.   are told they will be punished
    d.   all of the above

17.   When 13-month-old Fred saw his mother crying, he offered her his soother as a way of trying to comfort her. Fred's behavior was likely motivated by the feeling of

    a.   empathic distress
    b.   guilt
    c.   narcissism
    d.   vicarious punishment

18.   Kohlberg's theory of moral development has been criticized as biased against women because

    a.   Kohlberg never examined the moral reasoning of women in his research
    b.   women's moral concerns are more likely to center on issues of care and responsibility, rather than justice
    c.   women's moral concerns are more likely to center on issues of justice rather than care and responsibility
    d.   men are very concerned with obeying the rules, whereas women are not

19.   In Erikson's theory, children who have difficulty with this stage may be highly self-critical or may become rigid and constricted as a way of dealing with impulses they have come to view as bad.

    a.   initiative vs. guilt
    b.   trust vs. mistrust
    c.   industry vs. inferiority
    d.   autonomy vs. shame and doubt

20.   According to Erikson, _____ occurs when an individual fails to develop a coherent and enduring sense of self, and has difficulty committing to roles, values, people, and occupational choices.

    a.   the midlife crisis
    b.   despair
    c.   identity confusion
    d.   stagnation

ANSWERS

FILL-IN EXERCISES

1. imprinting 2. base 3. three; five, six 4. maturational 5. secure 6. internal working 7. unresolved
8. socialization 9. authoritarian; permissive; authoritative 10. gender; learning   11. three 12. intimacy
13. neglected   14. social cognition 15. self-concept 16. perspective taking 17. gender identity; two
18. constancy 19. morality 20. constraint 21. conventional 22. information-processing 23. narcissistic
24. guilt 25. empathic 26. psychosocial 27. guilt; industry 28. negative identity 29. stagnation
30. integrity; despair

USING WHAT YOU HAVE LEARNED

1. No - Attachment *is* important. It is related to later social and academic competence, and may be
      influential throughout life, perhaps influencing adult attachment.
2. No - While disturbed attachment does predict later adjustment problems, this is not always the case,
      nor is attachment style unchangeable.
3. No - While maternal responsiveness is very important, it is not the only variable to affect attachment.
      Temperament and environmental factors also are important.
4. Yes- Temperament may be very important. The three infant temperaments – easy, difficult, and slow-
      to-warm-up – may correspond to secure, ambivalent, and avoidant attachment styles. Inborn
      timidity or fearfulness may also be related.

APPLICATION

1. identity versus identity diffusion   2. initiative versus guilt 3. industry versus inferiority 4. generativity
versus stagnation 5. identity versus identity diffusion 6. intimacy versus isolation 7. industry versus
inferiority 8. generativity versus stagnation   9. autonomy versus shame and doubt

SAMPLE TEST QUESTIONS

1.	d	11.	d
2.	c	12.	a
3.	c	13.	a
4.	c	14.	c
5.	a	15.	b
6.	b	16.	d
7.	c	17.	a
8.	a	18.	b
9.	c	19.	a
10.	b	20.	c

Chapter 15
Psychological Disorders

PART ONE: PRE-READ AND WORK
Outline and Learning Objectives

Pre-read this chapter's table of contents and end-of-chapter summary. Then, use the outline segment-by-segment to help you work through the chapter. Jot down your own questions, comments, and notes in the space provided. Make a note of key terms and of difficult areas that you will need to review (include page numbers). Then, answer the questions in the learning objectives section that follows. Check off those you are confident that you can answer well. Re-read the material in the text for the questions about which you are less confident. Record the important points from your reading in the space below each question.

OUTLINE

The Cultural Context of Psychopathology

Culture and Psychopathology

Is Mental Illness Nothing but a Cultural Construction?

Contemporary Approaches to Psychopathology

Psychodynamic Perspective

Cognitive-Behavioral Perspective

Biological Approach

Systems Approach

Evolutionary Perspective

Descriptive Diagnoses: DSM-IV and Psychological Syndromes

DSM-IV

Disorders Usually First Diagnosed in Infancy, Childhood, or Adolescence

Substance-Related Disorders

Schizophrenia

From Brain to Behavior: The Biology of Schizophrenia

Mood Disorders

A Global Vista: Depression on a Hopi Reservation

Anxiety Disorders

Eating Disorders

Dissociative Disorders

Personality Disorders

One Step Further: Are Mental Disorders Really Distinct?

Central Questions: When Nature Becomes Nurture

LEARNING OBJECTIVES

Upon completion of Chapter 15, you should be able to answer the following questions.

1.   How is psychopathology influenced by culture?

2.   What is labeling theory? How did the research Rosenhan conducted in mental institutions support this view of psychopathology?

3.   What criticisms have been voiced concerning both the "mental illness is a myth" and labeling theory approaches?

4.   What are the differences between neuroses, personality disorders, and psychoses?

5.   What are the three questions that comprise a psychodynamic formulation?

6.   How do the behavioral and cognitive approaches conceptualize psychopathology?

7.   How does the biological approach conceptualize mental disorders?

8.   How do psychologists with a family systems approach view psychopathology?

9.   How would psychopathology be explained by evolutionary psychologists?

10.   What are the five axes that make up DSM-IV's multiaxial system of diagnosis?

11. What are the similarities and differences between attention-deficit hyperactivity disorder (ADHD) and conduct disorder?

12. How do both genetic and environmental factors account for the findings that alcoholism runs in families?

13. What are the major characteristics of schizophrenia?

14. Describe the *positive* and *negative* symptoms of schizophrenia.

15. How does the dopamine hypothesis account for both the positive and negative symptoms of schizophrenia?

16. Discuss the evidence indicating that both biological and environmental factors contribute to schizophrenia.

17. What are the differences between major depressive disorder, dysthymic disorder, and bipolar disorder?

18. Discuss the contributions of genetic factors, neurotransmitters, and environmental factors to depression.

19. What are the four types of cognitive distortions or errors in depressive thinking described by Beck? Provide examples for each.

20. How does the psychodynamic view of depression differ from the cognitive view?

21.   How does culture influence the way people view and experience depression?

22.   Describe the symptoms of the following anxiety disorders:

Phobia

Social phobia

Panic disorder

Agoraphobia

Obsessive-compulsive disorder

Posttraumatic stress disorder (PTSD)

23.   How do genetic vulnerability, environmental factors, and stress contribute to anxiety?

25.   How does David Barlow's model explain the development of panic attacks?

26.   What are the characteristics of anorexia nervosa and bulimia? What are the roles of biological, environmental, and personality factors in the development of these disorders?

27   What are the symptoms of borderline personality disorder and antisocial personality disorder? What similarities and differences are there in the etiology of each disorder?

28   Why is it difficult to distinguish the roles of nature and nurture in the etiology of psychological disturbances?

PART TWO: REVIEW AND LEARN
Key Terms, Fill-In Exercises, Application and Using What You Have Learned

Before doing the exercises below, review the information you learned in this chapter. Reread the work you did in part one of this study guide chapter, plus the interim summaries and end-of-chapter summary in your textbook. Review any problem areas. Once you feel comfortable with the material, do the following exercises without referring to your notes or textbook. If you have difficulty with a term or question, mark it and come back to it. When you have finished an exercise, go back to your notes and the textbook to find the answers to the questions that gave you difficulty. Finally, check your answers (key terms against the textbook and the rest against the answer key).

KEY TERMS

Psychopathology   _____

_____

Labeling theory _____

_____

Neuroses   _____

_____

Personality disorders   _____

_____

Psychoses   _____

_____

Etiology_____

_____

Psychodynamic formulation   _____

_____

Cognitive-behavioral _____

_____

Diathesis-stress model _____

_____

Systems approach _____

_____

System _____

_____

Family systems model _____

_____

Family homeostatic mechanisms_____

_____

Family roles _____

_____

Family boundaries _____

_____

Family alliances_____

_____

Descriptive diagnosis _____

_____

Clinical syndromes _____

_____

DSM-IV _____

_____

Multiaxial system of diagnosis _____

_____

Attention-deficit hyperactivity disorder (ADHD) _____

_____

Conduct disorder _____

_____

Substance-related disorders _____

_____

Alcoholism _____

_____

Schizophrenia _____

_____

Delusions _____

_____

Hallucinations _____

_____

Loosening of associations _____

_____

Positive symptoms _____

_____

Negative symptoms _____

_____

Dopamine hypothesis _____

_____

Ventricles _____

_____

Expressed emotion _____

_____

Mood disorders _____

_____

Manic _____

_____

Major depressive disorder _____

_____

Dysthymic disorder (or dysthymia) _____

_____

Bipolar disorder _____

_____

Mania _____

_____

Unipolar depression _____

_____

Negative triad   _____

_____

Cognitive Distortions   _____

_____

Anxiety disorders   _____

_____

Generalized anxiety disorder   _____

_____

Phobia _____

_____

Social phobia _____

_____

Panic disorder _____

_____

Agoraphobia _____

_____

Obsessive-compulsive disorder _____

_____

Obsessions _____

_____

Compulsions _____

_____

Posttraumatic stress disorder (PTSD)   _____

_____

Anorexia nervosa   _____

_____

Bulimia _____

_____

Dissociation   _____

_____

Dissociative disorders   _____

_____

Dissociative identity disorder   _____

_____

Personality disorders   _____

_____

Borderline personality disorder   _____

_____

Antisocial personality disorder   _____

_____

FILL-IN EXERCISES

Fill in the word or words that best fit in the spaces below.

1.   Thomas Szasz argued that mental illness is a _____.

2.   Psychodynamic psychologists use information they gather about the patient to make a _____ _____, develop a set of hypotheses about the patient's personality structure and the meaning of the symptom.

3.   From a cognitive perspective, psychopathology reflects dysfunctional _____ that maintain dysfunctional behaviors and emotions.

4.   The _____-_____ model holds that people with an underlying vulnerability may exhibit symptoms under stressful circumstances.

5.   Systems theorists refer to the methods family members use to preserve equilibrium in a family as family _____ mechanisms.

6.   Family _____ are parts individuals play in repetitive family dramas, according to system theorists.

7.   In descriptive diagnosis, constellations of symptoms that tend to occur together are referred to as clinical _____.

8.   Attention-deficit hyperactivity disorder is characterized by _____, _____, and _____ inappropriate for the child's age.

9.   Attention-deficit hyperactivity disorder is more prevalent in _____ *(males/females)* than in _____ *(males/females)* .

10.   As in other Western countries, the third largest health problem in the United States today, following heart disease and cancer, is _____.

11.   Individuals with schizophrenia often suffer from _____ -- false beliefs firmly held despite evidence to the contrary.

12.   Perceptual experiences that distort or occur without an external stimulus, common in schizophrenia, are referred to as _____.

13.   _____ describes a loss of interest in pleasurable activities, characteristic of major depressive disorder.

14.   Individuals with _____ disorder often experience both depression and mania.

15. According to Beck, _____ _____ involve a depressed person's transforming neutral or positive information in a negative direction.

16. From a _____ perspective, depression cannot be isolated from the personality structure of the person experiencing it.

17. At any given point in time, about _____ percent of the population has at least one irrational fear or _____.

18. _____ are persistent irrational thoughts or ideas that cause distress and interfere with an individual's life.

19. According to David Barlow, as autonomic responses such as quickened pulse, pounding heart, and difficulty breathing become associated with the panic state through classical conditioning, people with panic disorders often develop a fear of _____.

20. Bulimia is characterized by a _____-and-_____ syndrome.

USING WHAT YOU HAVE LEARNED

Beck's approach to depression emphasizes cognitive errors in the reasoning of depressed individuals. Below are some hypothetical situations involving such errors. Provide the most appropriate label for each error.

1. A stranger approaching an individual on the sidewalk suddenly crosses the street and begins walking on the other side. The individual concludes "He thinks I'm awful and can't stand to walk near me."

2. After being turned down for one date, a depressed man concludes, "I'm unattractive to women and I'll never get a date."

3. Ignoring her grade of A- on the midterm exam, a student asked, "Why can't I do well in this course?"

4. After being pulled over for going 10 mph over the limit, a driver concludes "This is terrible, I'm going to lose my license!" When informed by the police that all he was getting was a warning ticket, he concluded "It's just as bad, they'll never let me renew my insurance after this!"

5. After three years of repair-free driving, George's car got a flat tire when he drove over a broken bottle. He said to his friend, "I should never have bought this stupid car. It's nothing but a lemon!"

APPLICATION

Identify the disorder that best describes the following fictitious examples.

1.   An 8-year-old boy is having troubles in school. He cannot sit still at his desk, has trouble focusing on class work, and impulsively calls out answers without putting his hand up. He's been getting into arguments and fights lately with other kids, although his teacher thinks it may be due to his negative feelings about school.

2.   A writer has periods where she produces so much work that her friends are amazed. She's on an emotional high during her productive periods, and can get by with only a couple of hours of sleep each day. But she has other periods when she can't seem to write anything; she can't concentrate; in fact, she often can't even get out of bed for days at a time. During these times, nothing interests her, even things she usually loves to do.

3.   A restaurant worker has a persistent fear that he has inadvertently contaminated the food he is preparing with a poisonous compound. He repeatedly throws out the food and starts from scratch, meticulously writing down every ingredient he adds to the meal.

4.   An individual is afraid to leave her house and travel to work because of a fear of experiencing a panic attack on the subway or at the office.

5.   A 25-year-old gets into trouble with the law repeatedly for stealing and destroying the property of innocent victims. When caught, he shows no remorse and no concern for the harm he has caused his victims. He is extremely charming, however, and easily finds new victims to con.

6.   A college student is extremely anxious about his "performance" in front of others and what others may be thinking of him. The problem is so intense that he often avoids attending classes, in case he might be called upon to answer a question in class.

PART THREE: TEST AND KNOW
SAMPLE TEST QUESTIONS

Test how well you have learned this chapter's material by answering the sample test questions. You may wish to mark your answers on a separate sheet of paper so you can reuse this test for exam review. Once you have completed the exam, check your answers and then go back to your notes and the textbook to review questions you found difficult.

1.   According to psychiatrist Thomas Szasz

    a.   mental illness is a myth
    b.   panic disorders represent a fear of fear
    c.   psychiatric illness is in the eye of the beholder
    d.   the symptoms of any individual are really indicative of disruptions in the individual's family

2.   Psychodynamic theorists distinguish among three broad classes of psychopathology

    a.   neuroses, anxiety disorders, and psychoses
    b.   affective disorders, personality disorders, and psychoses
    c.   dissociative disorders, personality disorders, and psychoses
    d.   neuroses, personality disorders and psychoses

3.   The descriptive approach embodied in DSM-IV tends to be most compatible with

    a.   a psychodynamic approach to psychopathology
    b.   a disease model of psychopathology
    c.   a cognitive-behavioral approach to psychopathology
    d.   the systems approach to psychopathology

4.   The prevalence of ADHD is estimated at _____ of school-aged children.

    a.   5%
    b.   10%
    c.   15%
    d.   50%

5.   Research suggests that some children with conduct disorder

    a.   are oversensitive to rewards and punishments
    b.   are subject to intense anxiety in social situations
    c.   are relatively unresponsive to conditioning
    d.   frequently display self-mutilating behavior

6.   Perhaps the best predictor of whether someone will develop alcoholism is

    a.   the presence of an anxiety disorder
    b.   a history of conduct disorder or antisocial personality disorder
    c.   the presence of a bipolar disorder
    d.   a family history of alcoholism

7.   The neurotransmitter that seems to be involved in schizophrenia is

    a.   dopamine
    b.   GABA
    c.   norepinephrine
    d.   acetylcholine

8.   One member of a pair of MZ twins is diagnosed with schizophrenia, while the other remains healthy. What are the chances that the offspring of the healthy twin will develop schizophrenia?

    a.   slim, since the parent does not have schizophrenia
    b.   about the same as the chances of anyone else in the general population
    c.   impossible to determine
    d.   about the same as the offspring of the twin with schizophrenia

9.   Too little dopamine in the circuit that projects from the midbrain to the prefrontal cortex is associated with the

    a.   negative symptoms of schizophrenia
    b.   mood fluctuations in seasonal affective disorder
    c.   low conditionability of individuals with antisocial personality disorder
    d.   false alarms associated with anxiety disorders

10.   A chronic, low-level depression lasting more than two years, interrupted by short intervals of normal moods is referred to as

    a.   seasonal affective disorder
    b.   dysthymic disorder
    c.   bipolar depression
    d.   anhedonia

11.   A _____ episode refers to a period of abnormally elevated or expansive mood.

    a.   schizophrenic
    b.   agoraphobic
    c.   manic
    d.   borderline

12.   Beck describes the negative triad as a negative outlook on

   a.   the past, present, and future
   b.   the self, family, and others
   c.   the world, self, and future
   d.   working, loving, and happiness

13.   Unlike cognitive theorists, who focus on faulty cognition, psychodynamic explanations of depression focus on

   a.   distortions
   b.   beliefs
   c.   roles
   d.   motivation

14.   Nightmares, flashbacks, hypervigilance, exaggerated startle responses, and psychological numbness are symptoms associated with

   a.   bipolar disorder
   b.   schizophrenia
   c.   obsessive-compulsive disorder
   d.   posttraumatic stress disorder

15.   Roughly 80% of patients suffering from panic attacks

   a.   describe a stressful, negative life event that coincided with their first attack
   b.   report a history of physical or sexual abuse
   c.   attribute negative or malevolent intentions to other people and expect abuse and rejection
   d.   experience extremely unstable interpersonal relationships

16.   What percentage of patients with anorexia are male?

   a.   10%
   b.   25%
   c.   50%
   d.   90%

17.   Disruptions in consciousness, memory, sense of identity, or perception are characteristic of

   a.   panic attacks
   b.   narcissistic personality disorder
   c.   borderline personality disorder
   d.   dissociative disorders

18.   Psychodynamic theorists argue that _____ originates in pathological attachment relationships in early childhood, which lead to attachment problems later in life.

        a.   borderline personality disorder
        b.   narcissistic personality disorder
        c.   obsessive-compulsive disorder
        d.   bulimia

19.   In explaining the development of antisocial personality disorder, both social learning and psychodynamic approaches implicate

        a.   the importance of a sexually abusive male relative
        b.   physical abuse, neglect, and absent or criminal male role models
        c.   the importance of both anxiety and mood disorders in the individual's family
        d.   a high incidence of expressed emotion in the individual's family

20.   Schizoaffective disorder refers to

        a.   a depressive syndrome that occurs primarily in the winter
        b.   a mixture of anxiety and depression
        c.   a disorder that involves attributes of both schizophrenia and psychotic depression
        d.   a disorder characterized by alternating cycles of elation and depression

ANSWERS

FILL-IN EXERCISES

1. myth 2. psychodynamic formulation 3. cognitions   4. diathesis-stress 5. homeostatic 6. roles
7. syndromes   8. inattention, impulsivity, hyperactivity 9. males; females 10. alcoholism 11. delusions
12. hallucinations 13. anhedonia 14. bipolar 15. cognitive distortions 16. psychodynamic
17. five; phobia 18. obsessions 19. fear 20. binge; purge

USING WHAT YOU HAVE LEARNED

1. personalization
2. overgeneralization
3. arbitrary inference
4. magnification
5. arbitrary inference

APPLICATION

1. attention-deficit hyperactivity disorder
2. bipolar disorder
3. obsessive-compulsive disorder
4. agoraphobia
5. antisocial personality disorder
6. social phobia

SAMPLE TEST QUESTIONS

1.	a	11.	c
2.	d	12.	c
3.	b	13.	d
4.	a	14.	d
5.	c	15.	a
6.	d	16.	a
7.	a	17.	d
8.	d	18.	a
9.	a	19.	b
10.	b	20.	c

Chapter 16
Treatment of
Psychological Disorders

PART ONE: PRE-READ AND WORK
Outline and Learning Objectives

Pre-read this chapter's table of contents and end-of-chapter summary. Then, use the outline segment-by-segment to help you work through the chapter. Jot down your own questions, comments, and notes in the space provided. Make a note of key terms and of difficult areas that you will need to review (include page numbers). Then, answer the questions in the learning objectives section that follows. Check off those you are confident that you can answer well. Re-read the material in the text for the questions about which you are less confident. Record the important points from your reading in the space below each question.

OUTLINE

Psychodynamic Therapies

Therapeutic Techniques

Varieties of Psychodynamic Therapy

Cognitive-Behavioral Therapies

Basic Principles

Classical Conditioning Techniques

Operant Conditioning Techniques

Modeling and Skills Training

Cognitive Therapy

Humanistic, Group, and Family Therapies

Humanistic Therapies

Group Therapies

Family Therapies

A Global Vista: Culture and Psychotherapy

One Step Further: Psychotherapy Integration

Biological Treatments

From Brain to Behavior: Psychotropic Medications

Antipsychotic Medications

Antidepressant and Mood Stabilizing Medications

Antianxiety Medications

Electroconvulsive Therapy and Psychosurgery

Evaluating Psychological Treatments

Pharmacotherapy

Psychotherapy

Central Questions: What Works for Whom?

LEARNING OBJECTIVES

Upon completion of Chapter 16, you should be able to answer the following questions.

1.   What are the two principles on which the psychodynamic approach to therapeutic change rests?

2.   What three techniques do psychodynamic psychotherapists use to bring about therapeutic change?

3.   What are the similarities and differences between psychoanalysis and psychodynamic psychotherapy?

4.   What are the four steps involved in systematic desensitization?

5.   What are the differences between counter-conditioning and extinction as explanations of how systematic desensitization works?

6.   How does flooding differ from graded exposure?

7.   How does participatory modeling work to alleviate fear responses?

8.   How is skills training useful in helping people with specific interpersonal deficits?

9.   In what ways are Albert Ellis's Rational-Emotive Therapy and Aaron Beck's Cognitive Therapy similar?

10.   What is Albert Ellis's *ABC theory* of psychopathology?

11.   What are the key assumptions of Gestalt therapy?

12.   How is the *"empty chair technique"* used by Gestalt therapists?

13.   What are the key assumptions of Rogers's client-centered therapy?

14.   In what ways does group therapy differ from individual therapy? What are some advantages of group therapy approaches?

15.   What is the focus of the *structural* and *strategic* approaches to family therapy?

16.   Compare how family-systems therapists, psychodynamic therapists, behavior therapists and cognitive-behavior therapists approach marital therapy.

17.   Why do some psychotherapists attempt to integrate therapies?

18.   What psychotropic medication is effective with each of the following disorders? How does each medication work, and what are the drawbacks to its use?

        Psychosis

        Depression

        Bipolar disorder

        Anxiety

19.   For what disorders is electroconvulsive therapy (ECT) effective? What are the pros and cons to the use of ECT?

20.   How are lobotomies accomplished? What are the consequences of this procedure?

21.   What common factors underlie all therapies and may contribute to similar outcomes despite their different approaches?

22.   How do efficacy studies and efficiency studies differ? Why are both needed to evaluate psychotherapy?

PART TWO: REVIEW AND LEARN
Key Terms, Fill-In Exercises, Application and Using What You Have Learned

Before doing the exercises below, review the information you learned in this chapter. Reread the work you did in part one of this study guide chapter, plus the interim summaries and end-of-chapter summary in your textbook. Review any problem areas. Once you feel comfortable with the material, do the following exercises without referring to your notes or textbook. If you have difficulty with a term or question, mark it and come back to it. When you have finished an exercise, go back to your notes and the textbook to find the answers to the questions that gave you difficulty. Finally, check your answers (key terms against the textbook and the rest against the answer key).

KEY TERMS

Insight _____

_____

Therapeutic alliance   _____

_____

Free association   _____

_____

Interpretation _____

_____

Resistance _____

_____

Transference _____

_____

Psychoanalysis _____

_____

Psychodynamic psychotherapy _____

_____

Cognitive-behavioral _____

_____

Behavioral analysis _____

_____

Systematic desensitization _____

_____

Exposure techniques _____

_____

Flooding _____

_____

Graded exposure _____

_____

Response prevention _____

_____

Participatory modeling _____

_____

Skills training _____

_____

Social skills training _____

_____

Cognitive therapy _____

_____

Automatic thoughts _____

_____

Rational-emotive therapy _____

_____

ABC theory of psychopathology _____

_____

Humanistic therapies _____

_____

Gestalt therapy _____

_____

Empty-chair technique _____

_____

Client-centered therapy _____

_____

Unconditional positive regard _____

_____

Group therapy _____

_____

Group process _____

_____

Self-help group _____

_____

Family therapy _____

_____

Genogram _____

_____

Marital (or couples) therapy _____

_____

Negative reciprocity _____

_____

Psychotherapy integration _____

_____

Psychotropic medications _____

_____

Antipsychotic medication   _____

_____

Tardive dyskinesia   _____

_____

Antidepressant medications   _____

_____

Tricyclic antidepressants   _____

_____

MAO inhibitors   _____

_____

Selective serotonin reuptake inhibitors (SSRIs)   _____

_____

Lithium   _____

_____

Benzodiazepines   _____

_____

Electroconvulsive therapy (ECT)   _____

_____

Psychosurgery   _____

_____

Meta-analysis   _____

_____

Client-centered therapy _____

_____

Unconditional positive regard   _____

_____

Group therapy _____

_____

Group process _____

_____

Self-help group _____

_____

Family therapy _____

_____

Genogram   _____

_____

Marital (or couples) therapy   _____

_____

Negative reciprocity   _____

_____

Psychotherapy integration   _____

_____

Psychotropic medications   _____

_____

Antipsychotic medication _____

_____

Tardive dyskinesia _____

_____

Antidepressant medications _____

_____

Tricyclic antidepressants _____

_____

MAO inhibitors _____

_____

Selective serotonin reuptake inhibitors (SSRIs) _____

_____

Lithium _____

_____

Benzodiazepines _____

_____

Electroconvulsive therapy (ECT) _____

_____

Psychosurgery _____

_____

Meta-analysis _____

_____

Common factors   _____

_____

Efficacy studies _____

_____

Effectiveness studies   _____

_____

FILL-IN EXERCISES

Fill in the word or words that best fit in the spaces below.

1.   Understanding one's own psychological processes is referred to as _____.

2.   In psychodynamic treatment, the patient has to feel comfortable enough with the therapist in order to speak about emotionally significant experiences, a phenomenon called the therapeutic _____.

3.   _____ refers to barriers to free association or treatment that the patient creates.

4.   _____ refers to the process whereby people experience similar thoughts, feelings, fears, wishes, and conflicts in new relationships as they did in past relationships.

5.   The procedure in which the patient gradually confronts a phobic stimulus mentally while in a relaxed state that inhibits anxiety is referred to as _____ _____.

6.   In the technique of _____, the patient confronts the phobic stimulus all at once. A modification of this procedure that involves presenting real stimuli that are increasingly intense is called _____ _____.

7.   _____ _____ training is a behavioral procedure that has been devised for people with specific interpersonal deficits such as social awkwardness or lack of assertiveness.

8.   Aaron Beck refers to the things people spontaneously say to themselves and the assumptions they make as _____ thoughts.

9.   According to Albert Ellis, patients can rid themselves of unhappiness if they learn to maximize their _____ thinking and minimize their _____ thinking.

10.   The core of Beck's therapy, like Ellis's, is challenging _____ distortions.

11.   To Gestalt therapists, understanding _____ one feels a certain way is far less important than recognizing _____ one feels that way.

12.   The *empty chair technique* is one of the best known procedures used by _____ therapists.

13.   Carl Rogers was among the first to refer to people who seek treatment as _____ rather than _____.

14.   Rogers stressed the curative value of _____, the process of becoming emotionally in tune with and understanding the patient's experience, without judging it.

15.   One of the oldest and best known _____-_____ groups is Alcoholics Anonymous.

16.   As in group and psychodynamic therapy, the focus of family therapy is often on _____ as well as on content.

17.   Negative _____ refers to the tendency of members of a couple to respond to negative comments or actions by their partner with negative behaviors in return.

18.   Some therapists choose and combine techniques from different approaches to fit the particular case, a practice referred to as _____ therapy, one strategy of psychotherapy integration.

19.   The most serious side effect of antipsychotic medications is a movement disorder called _____ _____.

20.   Antidepressant medications increase the amount of _____, _____ or both in the synapses and appear to reduce depression by correcting for depletion of these neurotransmitters.

21.   Benzodiazepines _____ *(increase / decrease)* the action of the neurotransmitter GABA.

USING WHAT YOU HAVE LEARNED

Identify the type of therapy and/or approach associated with each of the following procedures.

1.   A therapist places an empty chair in front of the patient and has him imagine his ex-girlfriend is in the chair. The patient tells her how he felt when she broke up with him.

2.   A therapist works with a client to help him grow and mature, to help him experience himself as he really is. The therapist helps him identify feelings and offers him a supportive environment, expressing an attitude of fundamental acceptance without any strings attached.

3.   A therapist trains a patient in deep relaxation. She then presents the patient with a hierarchically ordered sequence of stimuli that frighten him.

4.   A therapist trains a patient to examine her irrational beliefs and the role they play in causing a negative emotional response. He demonstrates to the patient the illogic in her beliefs and then teaches her alternative ways of thinking.

5.   A therapist works with the patient to develop a map of her family over four generations, looking for similarities between her current problems and problems in the family's past.

6.   A patient visits his therapist 3 times a week. He lies on a couch, while she sits behind him. Often she instructs him to say whatever comes to mind -- thoughts, feelings, images, fantasies, memories, or wishes -- and to try to censor nothing.

APPLICATION

Situation

A friend of yours has been having a bad time with anxiety. She's been experiencing severe episodes of panic, accompanied by hyperventilation, a racing heart beat, and feelings of dizziness. When the attacks occur, she's petrified, feeling certain that she's having a stroke. She feels sure that she's going to have a panic attack while driving the car and that she'll pass out, lose control of the car and kill herself and someone else. She feels safe only if she stays at home or close enough to home that she can quickly return there if an attack occurs. She's always checking her pulse, looking for "signs" that a panic attack is about to happen. She decides to ask her doctor to refer her for help.

Questions to Answer

1.   Based on what you've read in this chapter, what do you believe would be the most appropriate psychotherapeutic approach for her? Why?

2.   How would a therapist using this approach conceptualize her problems?

3.   What procedures would the therapist using this approach employ?

4.   Regardless of what approach her therapist follows, what important characteristics should he or she display?

5.   Suppose pharmacotherapy were recommended for her. What type of medication would likely be effective?

6.   What would be some of the drawbacks associated with pharmacotherapy alone?

PART THREE: TEST AND KNOW
SAMPLE TEST QUESTIONS

Test how well you have learned this chapter's material by answering the sample test questions. You may wish to mark your answers on a separate sheet of paper so you can reuse this test for exam review. Once you have completed the exam, check your answers and then go back to your notes and the textbook to review questions you found difficult.

1.   To bring about therapeutic change, psychodynamic psychotherapies rely on three techniques

      a.   empathy, interpretation, and analysis of transference
      b.   free association, interpretation, and collaborative empiricism
      c.   interpretation, response prevention, and unconditional positive regard
      d.   free association, interpretation, and analysis of transference

2.   Transference refers to

      a.   the process whereby people experience similar thoughts, feelings, fears, wishes, and conflicts in new relationships as they did in past relationships
      b.   the replacement of a conditioned fear response with relaxation in the process of systematic desensitization
      c.   how selective serotonin reuptake inhibitors (SSRIs) work at the synapse
      d.   the process by which the therapist models a desired behavior and gradually induces the patient to participate in it

3.   Although many therapists continue to practice behavior therapy (treatment based primarily on behaviorist learning principles), most who make use of learning principles today are _____ in their orientation.

      a.   humanistic
      b.   structural and strategic
      c.   cognitive-behavioral
      d.   eclectic

4.   The effectiveness of cognitive-behavioral therapies lies in their

      a.   ability to target highly specific psychological processes
      b.   use of empathy and unconditional positive regard
      c.   focus on the individual in the context of his or her family system
      d.   focus on helping the individual to express repressed feelings

5. According to the cognitive-behavioral approach, phobic responses, like all avoidance responses, are

     a. difficult to treat
     b. particularly resistant to extinction
     c. treatable by helping the patient gain insight into his or her own psychological processes
     d. treatable through the use of active procedures such as the empty-chair technique

6. A procedure in which the therapist demonstrates a behavior and then encourages the patient to engage in the same behavior is

     a. social skills training   b. graded exposure
     c. participatory modeling   d. counter-conditioning

7. The "C" in Ellis's ABC theory of psychopathology refers to

     a. belief systems
     b. emotional consequences
     c. activating conditions
     d. unconscious conflicts

8. Beck, like Ellis, views cognitive therapy as a process of _____ , in which patient and therapist work together testing hypotheses.

     a. collaborative empiricism
     b. counter-conditioning
     c. experiencing one's true self
     d. growing and maturing

9. The goal of humanistic therapies is to

     a. help people understand the internal workings of their mind and thus gain the capacity to make conscious, rational, adult choices
     b. change maladaptive behavior patterns
     c. help people to a realization of the role their thoughts play in emotional or mental unhappiness, ineffectuality, and disturbance
     d. help people get in touch with their feelings, with their "true selves," and with a sense of meaning in life

10. One of the most widely practiced humanistic therapies is

     a. the structural and strategic approach
     b. rational-emotive therapy
     c. family-systems therapy
     d. client-centered therapy

11.   In Rogerian therapy, the therapist creates a supportive atmosphere by demonstrating _____ .

    a.   love and respect for the client
    b.   a therapeutic alliance with the client
    c.   unconditional positive regard for the client
    d.   collaborative empiricism to the client

12.   Losing touch with one's emotions and one's authentic "inner" voice leads to psychological problems such as depression and anxiety, according to

    a.   Ellis's ABC theory of psychopathology
    b.   Gestalt therapy
    c.   Rogers's client-centered therapy
    d.   the Consumer Reports survey

13.   Self-help groups differ from other forms of group therapy in that they

    a.   are generally not guided by a professional
    b.   focus on a common issue or disorder
    c.   are insight-oriented rather than behaviorally-oriented
    d.   reduce the problem of transference as there is no leader

14.   One of the most important contributions of Paul Wachtel's integrative approach is the notion that people's fears and expectations create self-reinforcing behaviors that often lead them to get precisely what they fear. This concept is known as:

    a.   negative reciprocity
    b.   learned helplessness
    c.   cyclical psychodynamics
    d.   response prevention

15.   Antipsychotic medications are also sometimes called

    a.   benzodiazepines
    b.   selective serotonin reuptake inhibitors (SSRIs)
    c.   monoamine oxidase (MAO) inhibitors
    d.   major tranquilizers

16.   Antipsychotic medications inhibit the action of

    a.   monoamine oxidase
    b.   dopamine
    c.   serotonin
    d.   norepinephrine

17. Tricyclic antidepressants

    a. block reuptake of serotonin and norepinephrine into the presynaptic membrane
    b. keep the chemical monoamine oxidase from breaking down neurotransmitter substances in the presynaptic neuron, making more neurotransmitter available for release into the synapse
    c. target serotonin rather than norepinephrine
    d. are the treatment of choice for bipolar disorder

18. Fluoxetine (Prozac) is the best known

    a. benzodiazepine
    b. antipsychotic
    c. selective serotonin reuptake inhibitor
    d. benzodiazepine

19. The main side effect of electroconvulsive therapy (ECT) is

    a. memory loss
    b. loss of sexual desire
    c. dry mouth, restlessness, agitation
    d. weight gain, nausea, light-headedness

20. ECT can sometimes be useful in treating _____, as well as depression.

    a. anorexia
    b. schizophrenia
    c. mania
    d. antisocial personality disorder

ANSWERS

FILL-IN EXERCISES

1. insight 2. alliance 3. resistance 4. transference 5. systematic desensitization 6. flooding; graded exposure 7. social skills 8. automatic 9. rational; irrational 10. cognitive 11. why; that 12. Gestalt 13. clients; patients 14. empathy 15. self-help 16. process 17. reciprocity 18. eclectic 19. tardive dyskinesia 20. norepinephrine, serotonin 21. increase

USING WHAT YOU HAVE LEARNED

1. Gestalt therapy (humanistic approaches)
2. client-centered therapy (humanistic approaches)
3. systematic desensitization (behavior therapy)
4. rational-emotive therapy (cognitive therapy)
5. family therapy (genogram)
6. psychoanalysis (psychodynamic approaches)

APPLICATION

1. Cognitive-behavior therapy. Its effectiveness for anxiety is well established.
2. Panic attacks are the result of associating autonomic reactions with an impending panic attack, leading to panic whenever these reactions occur. Feelings of helplessness in the face of an impending attack, and catastrophic thoughts about consequences compound the problem. Staying at home is the result of avoidance learning.
3. Paced breathing exercises; repeated exposure to experience of racing heart; rational analysis of the accuracy of catastrophic beliefs.
4. Empathy; warm therapist-client relationship; instilling a sense of hope and efficacy.
5. Benzodiazepines or antidepressants.
6. Possible physiological or psychological dependency.

SAMPLE TEST QUESTIONS

1.	d	11.	c
2.	a	12.	b
3.	c	13.	a
4.	a	14.	c
5.	b	15.	d
6.	c	16.	b
7.	b	17.	a
8.	a	18.	c
9.	d	19.	a
10.	d	20.	c

Central Questions: Social and Nonsocial Cognition

LEARNING OBJECTIVES

Upon completion of Chapter 17, you should be able to answer the following questions.

1.   Differentiate between attitude strength and attitude accessibility.

2.   Explain what is meant by the following components of attitudes: cognitive complexity, attitudinal ambivalence, and attitudinal coherence.

3.   Why aren't attitudes strongly predictive of behavior?

4.   Under what circumstances are the central and the peripheral routes to persuasion more persuasive, according to the elaboration likelihood model?

5.   Discuss each of the following components of persuasion distinguished by psychologists: source, message, channel, context, receiver.

6.   What is the phenomenon of cognitive dissonance?

7.   How do perception of choice and size of rewards and punishments influence the extent to which cognitive dissonance arises?

8.   How do self-perception theory and self-presentation account for the phenomenon of cognitive dissonance?

9.   Can it be said that cognitive dissonance is a culturally universal phenomenon?

10.   How have changing concepts of representation in cognitive science affected how psychologists view social cognition?

11.   In what ways does attractiveness influence first impressions?

12.   What is the role of schemas in the processing of social information?

13.   How do stereotypes lead to prejudice?

14.   How does the notion of the authoritarian personality explain prejudice?

15.   What is implicit racism, and how does this differ from a person's explicit attitudes?

16.   How can prejudice result from ingroup-outgroup distinctions?

17.   Why is contact alone insufficient to reduce intergroup hostility?

18.   What are three types of information people use in making internal or external attributions for behavior?

19.   How do discounting and augmentation influence attributions?

20.   What is the correspondence bias and how does it influence attributions?

21.   How can self-serving biases result in inaccurate social-information processing?

22.   What factors can cause biases in processing social information?

23.   What is the difference between the self as subject and self as object?

24.   Discuss the psychodynamic notion of self-representation.

25.   What are the emotional and physical consequences of discrepancies between (a) actual self and ideal self and (b) actual self and ought self?

26.   What is self-esteem? How do people with high self-esteem differ from those with low self-esteem?

27.   How can the concept of "self" be considered culturally relative?

28.   In what four major ways does social cognition differ from nonsocial cognition?

PART TWO: REVIEW AND LEARN
Key Terms, Fill-In Exercises, Application and Using What You Have Learned

Before doing the exercises below, review the information you learned in this chapter. Reread the work you did in part one of this study guide chapter, plus the interim summaries and end-of-chapter summary in your textbook. Review any problem areas. Once you feel comfortable with the material, do the following exercises without referring to your notes or textbook. If you have difficulty with a term or question, mark it and come back to it. When you have finished an exercise, go back to your notes and the textbook to find the answers to the questions that gave you difficulty. Finally, check your answers (key terms against the textbook and the rest against the answer key).

KEY TERMS

Upon completion of Chapter 17, you should be able to define the following terms.

Attitude _____

_____

Attitude strength_____

_____

Attitude accessibility   _____

_____

Implicit attitudes_____

_____

Attitudinal ambivalence   _____

_____

Attitudinal coherence   _____

_____

Persuasion   _____

_____

Central route _____

_____

Peripheral route _____

_____

Elaboration likelihood model _____

_____

Attitude inoculation _____

_____

Foot-in-the-door technique _____

_____

Cognitive dissonance _____

_____

Self-perception theory _____

_____

Self-presentation _____

_____

Social cognition _____

_____

First impressions _____

_____

Halo effect _____

_____

Stereotypes _____

_____

Prejudice _____

_____

Discrimination _____

_____

Authoritarian personality _____

_____

Ingroups _____

_____

Outgroups _____

_____

Attribution _____

_____

External attribution _____

_____

Internal attribution _____

_____

Consensus _____

_____

Consistency _____

_____

Distinctiveness _____

_____

Discounting _____

_____

Augmentation _____

_____

Correspondence bias _____

_____

Self-serving bias _____

_____

Self _____

_____

Self-concept _____

_____

Self-esteem _____

_____

Self-representations _____

_____

Self-schema _____

_____

Actual self _____

_____

Ideal self   _____

_____

Ought self   _____

_____

Self-consistency   _____

_____

FILL-IN EXERCISES

Fill in the word or words that best fit in the spaces below.

1.   The statement "alcohol leads to major social problems" is an example of the _____ component of an attitude.

2.   Attitudinal _____ refers to the extent to which a given attitude object is associated with conflicting evaluative responses.

3.   Deliberate efforts to change an attitude are referred to as _____.

4.   According to the elaboration likelihood model, _____ appeals to persuasion are more effective when the person both is motivated to think about a topic and has the time to consider the arguments.

5.   Building up an individual's resistance to persuasion, by presenting weak arguments that are easily countered is referred to as _____ _____.

6.   The _____ technique operates on the principle that once people comply with a small request, they are more likely to comply with a bigger one.

7.   _____ _____ occurs when a person experiences a discrepancy between an attitude and a behavior, or between an attitude and a new piece of information.

8.   _____-_____ theory holds that individuals infer their attitudes, emotions, and other internal states by observing their own behavior.

9. Social _____ refers to the processes by which people make sense out of themselves, others, social interactions, and relationships.

10. _____ are characteristics attributed to people based on their membership in specific groups.

11. Adorno and his colleagues identified what they called the _____ _____, characterized by a tendency to hate people who are different or downtrodden.

12. Prejudice requires a distinction between _____ and _____, that is, people who belong to the group and those who do not.

13. People tend to perceive members of _____ as much more homogeneous than they really are and to emphasize the individuality of _____ members.

14. The process of inferring the causes of one's own and others' mental states and behaviors is referred to as _____.

15. The extent to which a person always responds in the same way to the same stimulus, referred to as _____, is one of several types of information that are important in attribution judgments.

16. Increasing an internal attribution for behavior, despite situational demands, is referred to as _____.

17. _____ bias refers to people's tendency to see themselves in a more positive light than others see them.

18. Self as _____ refers to the person's experience of self as a thinker, feeler, and actor, whereas self as _____ is the person's view of himself or herself.

19. Hopes, aspirations, and wishes that define the way a person would like to be, make up the _____ _____.

APPLICATION

Situation

Ms. Beagley is having some problems in her grade-7 class. Two cliques of girls have formed. These cliques have become increasingly hostile toward one another, with taunting, name calling, and verbal aggression on the rise. In her attempt to solve the problem, Ms. Beagley has rearranged the seating in her classroom, so that girls from each clique must be seatmates. So far, this hasn't worked. Instead, hostilities seem to have increased. When one girl accidentally spilled her seatmate's coke at lunch, she was immediately accused of doing it on purpose. "You and all your friends are the same. You're jerks!" she was told by her seatmate. When the same girl offered her science book to her seatmate who had forgotten hers, her seatmate's response was, "What choice did she have, teacher would've made her loan it to me anyway!" Ms. Beagley cannot figure out what is happening in her class. She calls upon you to help her understand why these girls are so antagonistic to one another and to brainstorm with her for ways to solve this problem.

Questions to Answer

1.   From what you've read in Chapter 17, what do you think is going on in Ms. Beagley's class?

2.   What process do you think is at the root of the hostility and discrimination between these two groups of girls?

3.   What kind of errors or overgeneralizations can you see in how the girls in one clique view those in the other? How would you expect them to interpret positive and negative actions performed by members of their clique? How would they interpret the same behaviors performed by members of the other clique?

4.   Why hasn't Ms. Beagley's strategy of rearranging the seating plan been successful in resolving the hostilities? What would be a better way to reduce hostilities between the groups of girls?

USING WHAT YOU HAVE LEARNED

Provide the correct label for the phenomena described in each of the following:

1.   Joanne is an extremely attractive woman. She is a tall, slim, well-dressed business woman. When they first meet her, most people automatically assume that she must be competent and confident.

2.   Bill's car broke down at a busy intersection. As he sat there helplessly, motorists behind him began honking and shouting things at him like: "You jerk, why are you trying to hold up all the traffic?" "What's your problem? Do you enjoy making people late for work?"

3.   After hearing a vignette about a criminal attorney, most subjects recalled that he was shrewd and calculating, but few remembered the color of his briefcase.

4.   Hearing about the success of a gifted musician, whose father was also a very successful musician, one individual argued: "Oh well, she didn't have to work at it very hard. She's riding on her father's coat tails."

5.   Steve had to choose between psychology and dentistry. It was tough. He thought about it for a long time and then chose psychology. Afterward, he was told that dentists make a lot more money, and he began to ruminate about his choice. Then, he came across an article on the high incidence of stress-related illness in dentists. To ease his mind about his choice of psychology, he began reading all he could find about the stress dentists are under.

PART THREE: TEST AND KNOW
SAMPLE TEST QUESTIONS

Test how well you have learned this chapter's material by answering the sample test questions. You may wish to mark your answers on a separate sheet of paper so you can reuse this test for exam review. Once you have completed the exam, check your answers and then go back to your notes and the textbook to review questions you found difficult.

1.   Social psychologists distinguish the following three components of an attitude

    a.   cognitive, evaluative, behavioral
    b.   conscious, unconscious, preconscious
    c.   cognitive, social, physical
    d.   self-concept, self-esteem, self-representation

2.   The best form of persuasion when an attitude is not strongly held and is based on minimal knowledge is to

    a.   induce the person to think carefully and weigh the arguments
    b.   encourage emotional responses that bypass the belief components of the attitude
    c.   overwhelm the person with so much information that he or she no longer even knows what the issue is
    d.   offer tangible incentives to the person to change her opinion

3.   Which of the following characteristics of a speaker play an important role in how successful her attempt at persuasion will be?

    a.   credibility
    b.   attractiveness
    c.   power
    d.   all of the above

4.   The "foot-in-the-door" technique is based on the principle that

    a.   if the person delivering a message shows obvious pain (as though her foot were caught in the door), the listener will have sympathy with her and will comply with her request
    b.   if the person delivering a message can get the listener's clear attention, the listener is more likely to comply
    c.   once people comply with a small request they are more likely to comply with one that is bigger
    d.   if someone has complied with a big request, he will almost automatically comply with a smaller one

5.   After Bill bought his new, name-brand computer, he came across an advertisement for a clone that had all the features of his new computer and cost half the price. Bill began to collect all the information he could find on the value of buying a name-brand computer. Bill's behavior was motivated by

    a.   social cognition
    b.   cognitive dissonance
    c.   an intuitive scientist approach
    d.   a halo effect

6.   Jacob is an accountant with a busy practice. He is tall and athletic. Just seeing him pass by on the street, people "know" he's a good accountant. This inference people make about Jacob's abilities is known as a

    a.   self-serving bias   b.   correspondence bias
    c.   halo effect   d.   stereotype

7. When Julie heard that her doctor was a champion motocross rider, she just couldn't believe it. But, when she checked and found out it was true, she never forgot it. Motocross riding just does not fit in her _____ for doctors.

    a. context   b. attribution
    c. schema   d. implicit attitude

8. Which of the following is *not* true about social schemas?

    a. They facilitate recall of schema-relevant social information.
    b. They interfere with recall of information that is highly discrepant with the schema.
    c. They organize encoding of social information.
    d. They direct attention and guide the processing of social information.

9. Schemas about the personal attributes of a group of people that are often overgeneralized, inaccurate, and resistant to new information are referred to as

    a. implicit racism   b. prejudice
    c. discrimination   d. stereotypes

10. In attitudinal terms, _____ refers to the *evaluative* component of negative attitudes toward particular groups.

    a. stereotypes
    b. prejudice
    c. discrimination
    d. consensus

11. The _____ personality refers to a particular personality style that is prone to hate people who are different or downtrodden.

    a. antisocial
    b. authoritative
    c. borderline
    d. authoritarian

12. Jane Elliot's classroom study in which she informed children that brown-eyed children are superior and blue-eyed children are inferior clearly demonstrated how

    a. a distinction between ingroups and outgroups leads to prejudice
    b. social schemas can be altered easily by simply presenting information that conflicts with the content of the schema
    c. cognitive dissonance plays a major role in even the attitudes of school children
    d. children are resistant to information that they know is wrong, even when it's presented by an adult authority figure

13.   Islam and Hewstone's (1993) study of how Hindu and Muslim students in Bangladesh explained the causes of helpful or unhelpful behavior presented in vignettes revealed which of the following?

    a.   Helpful acts by ingroup members were attributed to environmental circumstances.
    b.   Helpful acts by outgroup members were seen to reflect enduring personality attributes.
    c.   Unhelpful acts by outgroup members were attributed to environmental circumstance.
    d.   Helpful acts by ingroup members were seen to reflect enduring personality attributes.

14.   The study of the conflict between the Rattlers and Eagles groups at a Boy Scout summer camp showed that

    a.   extended contact between the two groups (i.e., bringing the two groups together for pleasant activities) was what was required to reduce conflict
    b.   there was nothing that could reduce conflict between the two groups
    c.   conflict between the two groups could only be reduced by terminating the camp
    d.   cooperation and contact between the two groups were required to reduce conflict

15.   In making attributions to the person or to the situation, people rely on which of the following types of information?

    a.   stereotypes, ingroups, outgroups
    b.   consensus, consistency, distinctiveness
    c.   cause, effect, correlation
    d.   discounting, augmenting, attributing

16.   "I know what Jerry said to you was mean" said Phil, "but, let's give him a break. He just found out he failed all his midterms." Phil's attribution for Jerry's behavior shows evidence of

    a.   consensus   b.   augmentation
    c.   discounting   d.   consistency

17.   Correspondence bias refers to

    a.   looking for information that fits with the way a person already views him/herself
    b.   the effects of first impressions on our judgments of people
    c.   the belief people hold that positive qualities tend to cluster together
    d.   the tendency to attribute behaviors to people's personalities and to ignore possible situational causes

18.   A majority of people rate themselves above average on most dimensions. This is, of course, statistically impossible, and is a good example of:

    a.   self-serving bias   b.   correspondence bias
    c.   augmentation   d.   self-consistency

19. Emotions, such as fear, guilt, uneasiness, and self-contempt, which characterize anxious individuals, may the result of a discrepancy between

   a. ideal self and ought self
   b. actual self and ideal self
   c. actual self and ought self
   d. self as subject and self as object

20. Self-consistency refers to

   a. people's tendency to perceive themselves in a manner consistent with the view of those around them
   b. the ability to achieve a balance between the real, ideal, and ought selves
   c. people's tendency to behave in a consistent manner across a variety of situations
   d. people's tendency to interpret information to fit the way they see themselves and to prefer people who verify their view of themselves

ANSWERS

FILL-IN EXERCISES

1. cognitive (belief) 2. ambivalence 3. persuasion   4. rational   5. attitude inoculation 6. foot-in-the-door
7. cognitive dissonance   8. self-perception 9. cognition 10. stereotypes 11. authoritarian personality
12. ingroups, outgroups 13. outgroups; ingroup   14. attribution 15. consistency 16. augmentation
17. self-serving 18. subject; object   19. ideal self

APPLICATION

1. Intergroup antagonism and prejudice
2. Ingroup-outgroup distinction
3. They perceive members of the outgroup as much more homogeneous than they really are. They make the following attribution errors in explaining the behavior of outgroup members: When considering the behavior of those not in their clique (i.e., outgroup members) the girls attribute positive behavior (one girl offering to share her book) to environmental circumstances and negative behavior (spilling the coke) to internal personality attributes. Most likely they would attribute positive and negative behaviors performed by *ingroup* members to internal and external causes, respectively.
4. As was the case in the study with the Rattlers and Eagles at a boy scout camp, contact alone is not enough to resolve conflict. The contact must also involve cooperation. Ms. Beagley should create a situation that involves superordinate goals that require the two groups to cooperate for the benefit of all.

USING WHAT YOU HAVE LEARNED

1. halo effect   2. correspondence bias 3. social schema 4. discounting 5. cognitive dissonance (postdecision dissonance reduction)

SAMPLE TEST QUESTIONS

1.	a	11.	d
2.	b	12.	a
3.	d	13.	d
4.	c	14.	d
5.	b	15.	b
6.	c	16.	c
7.	c	17.	d
8.	b	18.	a
9.	d	19.	c
10.	b	20.	d

Chapter 18
Interpersonal Processes

PART ONE: PRE-READ AND WORK
Outline and Learning Objectives

Pre-read this chapter's table of contents and end-of-chapter summary. Then, use the outline segment-by-segment to help you work through the chapter. Jot down your own questions, comments, and notes in the space provided. Make a note of key terms and of difficult areas that you will need to review (include page numbers). Then, answer the questions in the learning objectives section that follows. Check off those you are confident that you can answer well. Re-read the material in the text for the questions about which you are less confident. Record the important points from your reading in the space below each question.

OUTLINE

Relationships

Factors Leading to Interpersonal Attraction

Love

A Global Vista: Love in Cross-Cultural Perspective

Altruism

Theories of Altruism

Bystander Intervention

Aggression

Violence and Culture

Violence and Gender

The Roots of Violence

From Brain to Behavior: Biological Foundations of Aggression

Social Influence

Obedience

Conformity

Group Processes

Central Questions: Individuals, Groups, and the Nature of Human Nature

LEARNING OBJECTIVES

Upon completion of Chapter 18, you should be able to answer the following questions.

1. How does each of the following factors influence interpersonal attraction: proximity, interpersonal rewards, similarity, and physical attractiveness?

2. What are the differences between passionate love and companionate love?

3. What are the differences in "sexual strategies" of males and females, as described by the evolutionary perspective?

4. How do attachment theorists view romantic love?

5. How do the concepts of love and marriage differ across cultures?

6. What are some of the characteristics of people in stable, long-term relationships?

7. How does the notion of ethical hedonism explain altruism?

8. What do evolutionary psychologists mean by reciprocal altruism?

9. How does the presence of others influence bystander intervention?

10.   How do the prevalence and form of aggression vary by culture and gender?

11.   What are the similarities and differences between the psychodynamic and evolutionary views of aggression?

12.   What neural and hormonal systems have been found to underlie aggressive behavior?

13.   How do television violence and pornography affect aggression?

14.   How does frustration lead to aggression? What environmental factors have been found to increase both aggression and frustration?

15.   What factors influence obedience, according to Milgram's research?

16.   How did Solomon Asch demonstrate the power of conformity?

17.   How do reference groups influence the norms to which people respond?

18.   How can people's attitudes and behavior be influenced by the roles they assume?

19.   What are several different roles that commonly emerge in groups?

20.   How do the following three leadership styles differ: autocratic, democratic, and laissez-faire?

21.   Explain the influence charismatic leaders hold over people.

PART TWO: REVIEW AND LEARN
Key Terms, Fill-In Exercises, Application and Using What You Have Learned

Before doing the exercises below, review the information you learned in this chapter. Reread the work you did in part one of this study guide chapter, plus the interim summaries and end-of-chapter summary in your textbook. Review any problem areas. Once you feel comfortable with the material, do the following exercises without referring to your notes or textbook. If you have difficulty with a term or question, mark it and come back to it. When you have finished an exercise, go back to your notes and the textbook to find the answers to the questions that gave you difficulty. Finally, check your answers (key terms against the textbook and the rest against the answer key).

KEY TERMS

Altruism_____

_____

Situational variables   _____

_____

Dispositional variables   _____

_____

Interpersonal attraction _____

_____

Social exchange theories   _____

_____

Passionate love _____

_____

Companionate love   _____

_____

Sexual strategies   _____

_____

Ethical hedonism   _____

_____

Reciprocal altruism   _____

_____

Bystander intervention   _____

_____

Diffusion of responsibility   _____

_____

Aggression   _____

_____

Instrumental aggression _____

_____

Frustration-aggression hypothesis   _____

_____

Social influence _____

_____

Social facilitation   _____

_____

Obedience   _____

_____

Conformity   _____

_____

Group   _____

_____

Norms   _____

_____

Reference groups   _____

_____

Status   _____

_____

Role   _____

_____

Task leader   _____

_____

Social-emotional leader   _____

_____

Leader   _____

_____

Charismatic leader   _____

_____

FILL-IN EXERCISES

Fill in the word or words that best fit in the spaces below.

1.   Helping another person with no apparent gain to oneself is referred to as _____.

2.   Social exchange theories hold that the foundation of relationships is _____ reward.

3.   Whereas _____ love is marked by intense physiological arousal and absorption in another person, _____ love involves deep affection, friendship, and emotional intimacy.

4.   According to evolutionary psychologists, short-term and long-term mating strategies are similar for _____ *(males/females)*.

5.   _____ _____ refers to the doctrine that all behavior, no matter how apparently altruistic, is designed to increase one's own pleasure or reduce one's own pain.

6.   _____ _____ holds that natural selection favors animals that behave altruistically if the likely benefit to each individual over time exceeds the likely cost.

7.   "_____ *of responsibility*" refers to a diminished sense of personal responsibility to act because others are seen as equally responsible.

8.   Calm, pragmatic aggression is referred to as _____ aggression.

9.   Electrical stimulation of the lateral _____ results in attack behavior in cats or rhesus monkeys.

10.   Although viewing pornography does not _____ sexual violence, viewing pornographic *aggression* does appear to _____ men to the brutality of sexual violence.

11.   Recent thinking suggests that frustration leads to aggression, to the extent that a frustrating event elicits an _____ emotion.

12.   Within countries as diverse as Spain, Italy, France, and the United States, the southern regions typically have the highest rates of _____ crime.

13.   Social _____ refers to the performance-enhancing effect of the presence of others.

14.   Milgram's research reveals that people will obey, without limitations of conscience, if they believe an order comes from a legitimate _____.

15.   Solomon Asch's research demonstrated the powerful influence of _____.

16.   Groups whose norms matter to an individual, and hence have an impact on the individual's behavior, are known as _____ groups.

17. A _____ is a position in a group that has norms specifying appropriate behavior for its occupants.

18. The _____ _____ is the group member who takes responsibility for seeing that the group completes its tasks.

19. In Kurt Lewin's study where groups of boys made crafts after school, the style of leadership that led to neither satisfaction nor efficiency was a _____ style.

20. A _____ leader is a leader who inspires obedience by the force of his or her personality.

APPLICATION

Situation

Jan is a 10th grader who has just moved to a new school, midway through the term. She immediately strikes up a friendship with Ruth, the girl whose locker is beside hers. Ruth doesn't appear to have many friends and seems to really enjoy Jan's company. During her first week at the new school, Jan had lunch with Ruth every day. As she gets to know the other girls, however, Jan discovers that nobody likes Ruth. Everyone agrees that it's not cool to be seen with Ruth, although nobody really knows why. As Jan feels more and more comfortable with her new classmates, she feels more and more pressure to reject Ruth. Sitting with some of her classmates one day, the conversation turns to Ruth. All the other girls agree that she's a "loser." Someone then asks Jan what she thinks about Ruth. She wants to stand up for Ruth, yet at the same time, she wants to be accepted by her new classmates. So she agrees that Ruth is a loser.[*]

Questions to Answer

1. What is the phenomenon underlying Jan's dilemma?

2. What factors lead to Jan's agreeing with the opinion of the group, despite her personal feelings to the contrary?

3. Would it make any difference if another classmate had stood up for Ruth before they asked Jan what she thought?

4. What is the term that would describe the unspoken rule among the girls in Jan's class that it's not cool to be seen with Ruth?

5. Why would this group of girls be labeled a *positive* reference group for Jan in view of their behavior?

---

[*] This situation was derived from Hanna, J. & Younger, A. (1991, April). *Peer rejection and conformity*. Paper presented at the biennial meeting of the Society for Research in Child Development, Seattle, WA.

USING WHAT YOU HAVE LEARNED

You have been asked to write a short article for the college newspaper on the topic of love and romance. The article is intended to dispel common myths and to present a psychological perspective on the topic. The editors want you to focus on the following points. Based on what you've read in Chapter 18, what would you say on each of these topics?

1.   What is it that attracts couples to each other?

2.   How important is physical attractiveness for love and romance?

3.   Are there different kinds of love?

4.   Are men and women looking for the same things in romance?

5.   How important is romance to marriage?

PART THREE: TEST AND KNOW
SAMPLE TEST QUESTIONS

Test how well you have learned this chapter's material by answering the sample test questions. You may wish to mark your answers on a separate sheet of paper so you can reuse this test for exam review. Once you have completed the exam, check your answers and then go back to your notes and the textbook to review questions you found difficult.

1.   Proximity, similarity, attractiveness, and degree to which an interaction is rewarding are factors that influence

   a.   interpersonal attraction
   b.   altruism
   c.   frustration, and, hence, influence aggression
   d.   leadership

2.   _____ is high at the beginning of a relationship, but tends to diminish over time, with periodic resurges or "peaks." On the other hand, _____ usually grows over time through shared experience.

   a.   intimate love; passionate love
   b.   passionate love; companionate love
   c.   physical love; emotional love
   d.   romantic love; compassionate love

3.   Attachment theorists argue that

    a.   insecurely attached infants will never be able to develop adult romantic relationships
    b.   while secure attachment in infancy is predictive of secure romantic relationships in adulthood, nothing can be predicted from insecure attachment relationships
    c.   adult romantic relationships are *not* related to mother-infant attachment
    d.   people pattern their romantic relationships on the mental models they constructed of earlier attachment relationships

4.   The notion that all behavior, no matter how altruistic it appears to be, is designed to increase one's own pleasure or reduce one's own pain is referred to as

    a.   ethical hedonism
    b.   reciprocal altruism
    c.   diffusion of responsibility
    d.   instrumental altruism

5.   Darley and Latane developed a multi-stage model of the decision-making process underlying bystander intervention. During stage 3, the presence of others

    a.   serves as an informational source (i.e., "is there a crisis here or isn't there?")
    b.   serves as a source of reassurance
    c.   serves to increase empathic distress in the bystander
    d.   leads to a diffusion of responsibility

6.   Most contemporary psychodynamic psychologists view aggression as

    a.   a basic instinct in humans
    b.   a class of behaviors that societies implant
    c.   an inborn behavioral potential usually activated by frustration and anger
    d.   behavior that is pleasurable only to sadists, delinquents, and antisocial personalities

7.   Across species, overt female aggression is largely elicited by

    a.   the mating attempts of a male when the female is unreceptive
    b.   competition between females for the same male
    c.   intrusion into their territory by another female
    d.   attacks on their young

8.   A number of studies have implicated low levels of _____ in aggression.

    a.   testosterone
    b.   serotonin
    c.   adrenaline
    d.   blood sugar

9.   Electrical stimulation of the _____ can result in aggression and hostility in humans.

    a.   gonads   b.   hippocampus
    c.   amygdala   d.   cerebellum

10.   Which of the following is likely *not* a result of watching violent television programs?

    a.   increased arousal   b.   increased inhibition
    c.   exposure to aggressive models   d.   desensitization to violence

11.   Violent crimes such as rape, assault, murder, as well as prison unrest peak

    a.   during the spring because of the increase in testosterone levels in men
    b.   during the summer months when it is hot
    c.   during the fall when the imminent onset of winter leads to frustration
    d.   during the winter when daylight hours are shortest

12.   Dollard and Miller proposed that when people become _____, they become aggressive.

    a.   frustrated   b.   obedient
    c.   charismatic   d.   hedonistic

13.   In Milgram's research which of the following led to a *decrease* in obedience?

    a.   the presence of confederates who gave incorrect answers
    b.   moving the experimenter to the same room as the subject.
    c.   moving the victim into the same room as the subject
    d.   all of the above

14.   If an adolescent shoplifts in order to be like her friends, her friends represent a

    a.   positive influence   b.   negative reference group
    c.   positive reference group   d.   social-emotional leader

15.   In Asch's research where subjects indicated which lines were of matching length

    a.   if even one of the confederates gave an incorrect answer, the majority of subjects conformed in their choices
    b.   if three or more confederates gave incorrect answers, the majority of subjects conformed in their choices
    c.   if three or more confederates gave incorrect answers, approximately half of the subjects conformed in their choices
    d.   if at least one confederate gave a different answer than the others, participants followed their own judgments most of the time

16. The group member who tries to keep the group working cohesively and with minimum animosity is referred to as the

    a. autocratic leader
    b. laissez-faire leader
    c. tension-release leader
    d. social-emotional leader

17. Zimbardo's research in which students played roles of prison inmates and guards showed that

    a. roles can actually influence social behavior
    b. because the roles were hypothetical, the students did not take them seriously
    c. roles have little influence on social behavior
    d. social behavior likely affects the roles people choose

18. In Kurt Lewin's study where groups of boys made crafts after school, the style of leadership that led to efficiency but also discontent was a _____ style.

    a. autocratic
    b. democratic
    c. laissez-faire
    d. permissive

19. The personality dimensions characteristic of successful leaders are

    a. extroversion and stubbornness
    b. extroversion, risk-taking, and friendliness
    c. persuasiveness, meekness, and cheerfulness
    d. extroversion, agreeableness, conscientiousness

20. A leader who inspires obedience by the force of his or her personality is referred to as

    a. a social-emotional leader
    b. an instrumental leader
    c. a charismatic leader
    d. a democratic leader

ANSWERS

FILL-IN EXERCISES

1. altruism 2. reciprocal 3. passionate; companionate 4. females 5. ethical hedonism 6. reciprocal altruism 7. diffusion 8. instrumental 9. hypothalamus 10. cause; desensitize 11. unpleasant 12. violent 13. facilitation 14. authority 15. conformity 16. reference 17. role 18. task leader 19. laissez-faire 20. charismatic

APPLICATION

1. *Conformity.* As in Asch's studies on judgments of line length, this situation involves an individual who is confronted with opinions that differ from hers. Jan likes Ruth. But her classmates agree that it's not cool to like Ruth. So Jan changes her opinion to conform to the group.

2. What led to it was amount of opposition and need for social approval. Jan is a new student who wants to be accepted into her new peer group. Because her classmates unanimously agree that it's not cool to be Ruth's friend, Jan suppresses her opinion that Ruth is her friend, and conforms to the group opinion to gain their approval.

3. Yes. In Asch's studies, if even one confederate allied himself with the subject, the participants were more likely to stick with their original opinion. If one classmate had stood up for Ruth, it is likely that Jan would have stuck to her original opinion about Ruth.

4. A *norm.* All groups develop norms, or standards for behavior. This group of girls has an unspoken standard that it is not cool to be seen with Ruth.

5. The group is a *positive* reference group because Jan tries to emulate its members and meet their standards.

SAMPLE TEST QUESTIONS

1.	a	11.	b
2.	b	12.	a
3.	d	13.	c
4.	a	14.	c
5.	d	15.	d
6.	c	16.	d
7.	d	17.	a
8.	b	18.	a
9.	c	19.	d
10.	b	20.	c